Redemptive

Monica Hailey Sharpe

Disclaimer

Redemptive

Copyright© 2019 by Monica Hailey Sharpe

This book is based on the author's life. Although names, places and circumstances have been changed and embellished to protect those involved the story is presented as fiction.

All rights reserved. No part of this book may be reproduced, stored in a retrieval system, or transmitted in any form or by any means – electronic, mechanical, photocopy, recording, or otherwise – without the written permission of the publisher, except for brief quotations in printed reviews.

ISBN: 978-0578529998

Printed in the United States of America

Burkwood Media Group, Inc.

P O Box 29448

Charlotte, NC 28229

Dedication

This book is dedicated to my dad,

the late

Robert Eugene Davis.

August 18, 1949 – November 19, 2013

Acknowledgements

I never expected to write a book. The journey through the process of telling this story and standing in my truth could not have happened without certain people who believed in me.

Eddie Lamar Sharpe, thank you for your love and support and putting up with me during this process.

My grandma, Ms. Annie Mae Hailey, who I love dearly. Thank you for loving me and your words of wisdom.

My aunt, Mrs. Shirley Hailey Baker, who has always been supportive of me.

My children, Sherita Hailey Funderburk and Christina Crosby, you two make my life so much better.

My mom, Mrs. Annie Benson, who continues to stretch me beyond my comfort zone.

My publisher, Debra Funderburk and her team at Burkwood Media Group, Inc.

Introduction

Monique Harper is one special woman. Have you ever met someone who seems to have it all together? This would be Monique. From handling her business, to keeping her family straight, right down to handling her man. But behind every strong exterior is an interior full of secrets, issues, and downright foolishness.

The Harper family is one complex bunch who despite their idiosyncrasies, remain connected. Just like any other family, they fight, cutup, backstab and betray, but at the end of the day will hurt someone if you hurt one of them.

This story is about the life and experiences of one woman just trying to make it in life. The challenges she face and the obstacles she must overcome will have you laughing, crying and rooting for her till the very end. You will understand after reading her story why

Redemptive is about finding your truth, dealing with it, and becoming better by it.

Chapter 1

The Attack

It had been a long and hectic day at work and all Monique could think of was going for a much-needed walk when she got home. Work had been extremely busy lately and although glad for the business, it didn't allow her much time to exercise. This was the day she was determined to walk. Besides she couldn't let her plastic surgery be in vain.

While pulling into her garage the phone rang. It never failed, as soon as someone thought she was home from work, the calls would start. Today was not any different. Grabbing her bags heading toward the door, phone still ringing, Monique just wanted to catch the last hour of the sun before it set. Finally, it stopped ringing, but immediately started again. This time she looked to see it was none other than her cousin Cyrus. The two were more like brother and sister than cousins, but Cyrus was as slick as his name and whenever he called, Monique knew drama was attached to it.

"Hey." She finally answered while walking to her bedroom to change into her exercise clothes.

"What took you so long to answer the phone?"

"I was just pulling in when you called. I wanted to get in the house and get ready for my walk."

"Did you talk to Aunt Geneva?"

"About what? What did Mama do this time?"

"I think you need to talk to her is all. This tension between the two of you is keeping me up at night."

"Take your ass to bed, Geneva will be fine, and I am going for my walk. I will talk to you later."

Before Cyrus could respond Monique hung up the phone and threw it on the bed. What she wasn't going to do was deal with her Mama telling her what she should and shouldn't do with her life. Yes, her life was complicated, but it was working for her just fine. Shaking her head in an attempt to forget the crazy conversation with her cousin, she grabbed her water bottle and headed out the back door to the walking trail.

Redemptive

The trail appeared empty which made her glad she didn't have to make small talk with anyone. All she wanted was alone time to gather her thoughts and decompress from the last couple of crazy weeks.

Monique picked up her pace in order to get three miles in before the sunset. Dusk was already starting to fall. At the two-mile mark, she took a water break. A noise caught her attention. Looking around the trail all she could see were the surrounding trees. Thinking it was all in her mind Monique began walking again. Remembering to take deep breaths the closer she got to reaching her goal, someone grabbed her from behind before she realized it. With a gloved hand over her mouth, it made it impossible for her to scream. "Don't panic, think," she said to herself. Her instincts kicked in and the self-defense classes she'd taken paid off in spades. Stomping on the attacker's foot and then his shin, he pushed her to the ground and stumbled off. She could hear the engine of a vehicle start on the other side of the path as she fell to the ground hitting her head on the concrete. Everything went black.

When Monique came to herself she wasn't sure how long she'd been out. It couldn't have been too long because it still wasn't dark yet. Pulling herself up while a bit disoriented she made her way home. Amar was in the kitchen finishing dinner. The close of the storm door caused him to turn in its direction.

"Hey babe, I was starting to get worried," he said while closing a lid on one of the pots. Looking at her more closely he saw blood dripping on her shirt. "What the hell happened to you?" Moving toward her to get a better look Amar could see a lump starting to form on her head. His answer about the blood was now apparent.

"I was attacked." Leaning on the counter for support, Monique was also trying to catch her breath and her balance.

"Attacked? Where? Here in this neighborhood? This is a safe neighborhood."

Before Monique could answer any question Amar was headed toward the door. Amar was normally a man of few words but when it came to family, he took being the protector very seriously.

"Amar, he's gone. I was able to fight him off but fell and hit my head. I heard the vehicle start but didn't see it.

Amar was correct in his assessment their neighborhood was safe. They'd lived there for more

Redemptive

than ten years and never heard of anything like this happening before.

"Let me take you to Urgent Care."

Heading to the stove to turn it off and reaching for his keys Amar heard Monique say, "No, I think I will be okay."

"What do you mean no? You just told me you hit your head. You might have a concussion. We're not about to play around with this. Get in the car."

"Can I change my shirt first, at least?"

Standing, looking at his wife, Amar knew he wasn't going to win that one. Didn't matter with her head already bleeding, no doubt would mess up a new shirt, but if that's what it took for her to get in the car, he would learn to pick his battles.

On the short drive to Urgent care, Monique's head began to throb. She wouldn't admit it to Amar but was glad he'd made her come. They didn't have to wait long before Monique was called back. The doctor was nice enough and thorough in her examination. She ordered an x-ray and was certain Monique had a minor concussion. "Rest for the next couple of days," the doctor ordered and wrote a prescription for Vicodin. The lump would go down in a few days and it was merely scraped, not needing any stitches. The nurse cleaned the wound before sending Monique home.

Later that night when the two were back home Monique could tell Amar was bothered by the incident. He was quieter than usual which made her concerned. When she came out the shower he sat on side of the bed with his head down looking defeated.

"I'm okay Amar. I don't want you to worry about what could have happened. I'm safe and it's over," said Monique trying to make him feel better.

"Is it?" He looked at her with one eyebrow raised.

"What do you mean? Yes, it's over."

"Somebody who may or may not live here attacked you on a walking trail that is exclusive to this neighborhood and you don't expect me to be concerned? My job is to protect you as much as I can. Besides that, what about the other people in this neighborhood? They have a right to know what happened so if nothing else they can be on the lookout."

"Do you think we should call the cops? Do you want them sniffing around here?"

Redemptive

"No, I don't but we can at least let the president of our Neighborhood watch know and they can send out the information on the community link.

"That'll work. Now can we both get some sleep. This has been one hell of a day."

"Let me fix you a plate. You need to eat something before you take your pain meds."

"Okay, but just a little something," said Monique while fluffing her pillows to get comfortable in the bed. While turning the covers on the bed back she saw her cell phone. Picking it up, there were twenty-two missed calls from her crazy family. Amar must have called them while she was being seen. "Not tonight family. You will have to wait until tomorrow."

Chapter 2

Memories

The pain pill didn't take long to kick in and Monique was glad. The last thing she remembered was Amar getting ready to say his last prayer for the evening. The first part of her sleep was great, but the fall must have jarred something because images flashed through her mind and interrupted the peacefulness. A man kept grabbing at her in the dream. At first she thought it was the attacker, but this was someone she knew, seemed familiar with at least, but couldn't quite make out the face. Apparently she was crying out in her sleep, because Amar was shaking her and telling her to wake up.

When she went to get up her head felt as someone had hit her with a brick. Swaying back and forth she decided to lie back down. Drenched in sweat and

Redemptive

trying to process what she saw in her dream, Monique blamed it on the concussion and the pain meds.

"What were you dreaming about?" Amar asked while rubbing his eyes.

"Hell if I know. It was some crazy mess for sure."

"Crazy how?"

"Don't ask me a bunch of questions this early, Amar. My head hurts and I'm still sleepy."

"You better be nice to me. Yo ass can't get up and do nothing so I'm all you got right now."

"You right. Can you get me a night shirt since this one is wet?"

Grumbling under his breath, Amar got up and got the shirt. "Do you need anything else while I'm up?"

"Maybe a bottle of water."

Without a word Amar went and got the water. Monique slowly tried to sit up to change her shirt. Still trying to process the dream, she couldn't figure out where it was coming from. It was not the time to talk to Amar about it because she didn't understand it yet. Telling herself it was just a dream, Monique waited for Amar to bring her water. When he returned he'd brought a tray with fresh fruit, a muffin, and her bottle of water. This is why she loved this man so much.

"Thanks babe, you're so good to me."

"And don't you forget it, either. How's your head?"

"I don't feel anything right now, so I'll say the meds are working."

"Good, maybe you'll let me get some sleep now." Returning to bed Amar did just that, got in the bed, position himself back to his sweet spot and went to sleep. Monique watched as he went through his ritual, chuckled and continued nibbling on her treats.

Amar was a man of few words, but when he spoke it was matter of fact and he was off to the next thing. Monique had learned to accept him for who he was beneath that gruff exterior. Little did she know when she'd stalked him years ago, they would have a future together. She wasn't sure exactly what it was, but something about him stirred something in her and felt it was worth pursuing. Their courtship turned into a serious relationship and before long the two married.

Her life before Amar was lived on her own terms, traveling, partying and having a good time. She never let a man use her. The man played by the rules she set, or he didn't play at all. For some reason it had been

Redemptive

different with Amar. One thing she would not do was admit that to him, it would give him too much satisfaction. But Monique loved him and their relationship worked. Like in any relationship it had taken time for them to set boundaries but once they were established they'd become a powerhouse couple. Her grandmother had been right when she told her she'd found the right one this time.

The family was divided regarding Amar. They either loved him or hated him. It didn't matter to Monique because it really wasn't their business. This was her life and it was working for her. Better yet, Amar could care less about whether anybody liked him or not.

This was Monique's second marriage. Her first marriage to Graham produced two children, her son Shane and her daughter Camille.

Her son Shane was the apple of her eye but like with most black males he had issues. Monique tried to help him, but he wanted to figure them out for himself. Amar would talk to him man to man about his issues and Shane would listen, but in the end wanted to do things his own way. When Shane married Tychia, Monique wondered if that was the best for her son since she came with her own set of baggage. Could they get through their individual issues to make their marriage work. Tossing and turning trying to stop the thoughts from running through her head like a herd of wild horses, she asked herself, *Why was she thinking about this foolishness at 1:00 in the morning*? Maybe it was because she didn't want to go back to sleep and fall into the darkness of that terrible dream.

Chapter 3

The Intrusion

Monique wasn't sure how long she'd been asleep when she heard Amar talking to someone on the phone. Telling whoever it was that it wasn't necessary for them to come over. He was working from home today and could get her whatever she needed. Slowly rising to sit on the edge of the bed, Monique needed to go to the bathroom but didn't want to make any sudden moves. Feeling the lump on her head while waiting for the courage to stand, it had gone down but was really sore. Amar walked into the room dressed and no doubt had already finished his morning prayers and was ready to start his day. His Muslim faith required him to pray five times a day and unaware of the time Monique was sure he'd prayed at least once so far.

"Morning," he said when he entered.

"Morning."

"I've been on the phone with everybody wanting to come over here."

"Uhm, no. I can't deal with anybody today."

"I know. I told them I was here. If we needed anything we would call."

"What I don't need is drama. You know they will find a way to make it about them."

Amar laughed. "What are you doing up?"

"I need to go to the bathroom."

"Let me help you up. You probably shouldn't try going on your own."

"Let me at least try." Monique tried to stand and immediately felt lightheaded. "Maybe it wasn't such a good idea after all." Waiting for Amar to say something smart, she offered him her hand. He didn't say one word and helped her to the bathroom. "I think I'll shower while I'm in here. Can you get me a change of clothes please?"

"What do you want?" he asked. Again, being true to his character as a man of few words.

"A pair of sweats and a t-shirt is fine."

Redemptive

A few minutes later Amar returned with her clothes. "What do you want for breakfast?"

"Grits and eggs, maybe a piece of toast."

"Okay. Finish doing what you need to do and then I'll go cook. I want to make sure you are out the shower before I leave out of here."

Monique turned the shower on, brushed her teeth and slowly made her way into the shower. The warm water awakened her senses and she felt refreshed. Closing her eyes to enjoy the water to fall over her body she began to sway slowly. A quick flash crossed her mind. It was a split second, but she recognized it. It was the same scene she saw in her dream. A man grabbing at her but she couldn't tell exactly what he was doing. Breathing rapidly, Monique held on to the wall of the shower. *What the hell was that?* she thought. Trying to catch her breath while steadying herself at the same time, she finished her shower, got dressed and made her way back to the bedroom.

"You good?" Amar asked when she returned to the bed.

"Yeah, I'm good."

"Then I'm going to fix your breakfast. Be back shortly."

"Okay."

Monique climbed in bed and turned on the TV. This was a good time to catch up on some of her trashy shows. Scrolling through the guide she looked for something good to watch. After making her selection she propped up her pillows to make herself comfortable. It wasn't too long before Amar returned with breakfast.

"That was quick," she said to him.

"How long does it take to cook some eggs and grits, Mon?"

Monique looked at him refusing to cutup early in the morning. Or was it early? She didn't know what time it was, but she would let it pass either way.

"Thanks."

"Uh huh." I'm going down the hall to the office. If you need me call me."

"Alright."

No sooner than Monique started to enjoy her breakfast, the doorbell rang. Who the hell can't follow orders, she thought. Whoever it is, is about to get their feelings hurt. How you gone come to somebody's house when you've been told not to? She couldn't even finish her breakfast now cause she was mad. When Monique heard the clacking of heels on the hardwood floor she

Redemptive

immediately knew who it was. Her over the top wanna be daughter-in-law. Where Shane found this girl, Monique was still trying to figure that out. The two got alone for the most part, but like her son, Tychia had her issues. Monique certainly was not ready for a visit from her right now. When she reached the bedroom Tychia dropped her bag on the floor by the bed making a loud thud as it hit and made her way to Monique.

"I know Amar said you didn't need company, but I told Shane I had to come over and see you." Moving Monique's tray from in front of her, Tychia leaned over to hug her. Smelling like she fell into a bottle of cheap perfume Monique tried her best not to cough from the overwhelming scent.

"I appreciate the concern but why are you not at work?" asked Monique as she pulled a strand of hair from her mouth from Tychia's hair.

"Now Moni, you know I wouldn't be able to concentrate knowing you were over here hurt," her daughter-in-law said as she flopped on the bed beside Monique.

"See that's what I'm talking about right there. Why are you so concerned about me Ty when you should be worried about your own business? I appreciate it, don't get me wrong, but you know you need to have your ass at work."

"You worry too much, Moni. It's all good." Ty grabbed the tray to take in the kitchen.

"How you know I was finished with that?"

"Please, these grits are cold," Tychia said while she strutted out the room heading toward the kitchen."

Monique grabbed her phone to call Amar. When he answered, she told him to get rid of her. "Not today Amar, not today." She could hear Amar talking to her but couldn't hear his words. It wasn't long before Ty came in the room, her normal bubbly self acting like Amar didn't just finish talking to her.

"I'm not going to be able to stay after all, Moni. Something has come up and I need to go take care of it, but I will call you later."

Monique looked at her as she gathered her things. This girl truly lives in her own world, she thought to herself. "Okay Ty, call Amar's phone in case I'm asleep." Ty kissed her on the cheek and was gone.

"I want that girl to get her life together. Maybe one day." Monique turned over in the bed and started back watching her trashy TV show.

Chapter 4

Monique & Amar

It was later in the day when Monique opened her eyes and looked at the clock. Amar must have turned the TV off because the room was quiet. She laid for a few more minutes before attempting to get up. This time she was able to get to the bathroom without feeling lightheaded. The lump had gone down on her head but not completely. This was a good sign she felt. When she finished in the bathroom she made her way down the hall to check on Amar. He was on the phone and she could tell by the conversation it was work related. She sat in a chair across from his desk. The bright sunlight from the window was bright and so she moved her chair to avoid it.

"I'll call you back," Amar told the person on the other end of the phone. Looking at Monique trying to move a chair was enough to get his attention.

"What are you doing?"

"The sun was too bright."

"So that means you ain't supposed to be in here."

"I'm feeling better. My head doesn't hurt, the lump is going down, and I'm hungry."

"I grilled steaks earlier and baked some potatoes and made a salad."

"Everything good at work?"

"Yep, everything is good. Come let me get your plate ready."

"I told you I was feeling better; I can get it."

Amar simply gave her a look and without another word she followed him in the kitchen. Monique sat at the breakfast table while Amar brought her plate. He sat with her as she ate, filling her in on the phone calls while she slept.

"Geneva is coming over when she gets off work." Amar fumbled with moving dishes around to avoid eye contact.

Monique dropped her fork. "Why? I thought you were handling this?" she asked sounding anxious.

"She's your mother……."

Redemptive

Before Amar could finish the sentence, Monique simply said, "And?"

"And you know she would want to come over. Listen, whatever is going on with you two will have to be addressed at some point, but today she is coming over. I will make sure she doesn't stay long, but allow her this Mon."

"Fine. But I'm warning you, if she comes out of her mouth wrong, I'm gonna go off."

"No…..you're not. Not today. Save it for another day. Now finish your food before it gets cold."

Monique picked up her fork and continued to eat. Looking at Amar all she could think about was, who was he to tell me…..but she decided to play nice for now and told him the food was really good. By the time she finished lunch she was tired and headed back to bed. She didn't take a pain pill this time, just crawled in the bed and tried to find the show she'd started watching earlier. Looking at the clock she had three hours before her mother would be there. She needed every second of that time to get herself together for that visit.

The nightmare invaded Monique's sleep once again, but this time it was more vivid. She recognized the man in the dream and it caused her to scream. The next thing Monique knew was Amar waking her from her sleep.

"Dreaming again?" he asked when she woke from her sleep still slightly disoriented.

Looking at him with tears in her eyes, Monique said, "I don't think it's a dream, I think it really happened."

"What really happened?" he sat on the side of the bed holding his wife. Talk to me Mon, he whispered.

"I was molested."

Chapter 5

Another Intrusion

Before Monique could tell Amar the details of the dream now turned reality, the doorbell rang. They both looked at each other, sitting motionless. The doorbell rang again.

"Are you going to be okay?" asked Amar.

"I don't know."

"Should I tell her this is not a good time after all?"

"No, let her go ahead and come in, what I don't need is additional drama right now, but let's both agree, thirty minutes and she's gone."

"Agreed."

Amar went to answer the door. When he opened it, there stood Geneva and Cyrus. Before Amar could say anything, Geneva came in the door explaining.

"Amar, I know Monique would want to see Cyrus, you know how close they are. It'll be alright," she said while making her way in.

Geneva was a complicated woman who was always stirring somebody else's pot but couldn't manage her own.

Amar took a deep breath while stooping to greet his mother in law. He then shook Cyrus' hand and led them to the bedroom. Monique met them in the hallway.

"Hey y'all, let's sit in the den."

"Hey Monique, should you be up and moving around?" asked Geneva walking toward Monique to give her support.

"I'm good, Geneva. The den is fine. Surprised to see her cousin, Monique addressed him, "I didn't know you were coming, Cyrus."

Redemptive

"Girl, after Aunt Geneva said she was coming over, you know I had to come too. You know I had to make sure you were good for myself. Now tell us what happened and don't leave out any details," Cyrus said as he took his seat in a side chair in the den.

"There is nothing to tell really, I was on the walking trail, I heard a noise, but nobody was on the trail but me, next thing I knew someone grabbed me from behind and I went into self-defense mode. The person ran through the woods and I heard the car leave before falling and hitting my head."

"So you didn't see him?" asked Geneva.
"I just said Geneva, he grabbed me from behind," Monique answered in a very agitated voice. Geneva ignored her daughter's tone and continued assessing the situation.
"Good thing you and Cyrus took those classes. Anything could have happened. And to think it happened out here in this neighborhood."

"Girl, I felt bad when I heard the news. I had just talked to you. I can't believe that happened to you. But I'm glad you okay."

Monique sat looking at the two of them. *Thick as thieves, always plottin' or scheming about something.* All she could think was what were they up to next. Before she could respond to either, Amar offered them something to eat, knowing they wouldn't turn it down, while Monique eyed him as a reminder they only had thirty minutes to be there. Amar completely ignored the gesture. Once they fixed their plates, they picked up where they left off in the conversation.

"What did the doctor say Monique?" Cyrus started the questions this time.

At 5'8 Cyrus was on the thin side for his height. He and Monique grew up together when his mother died, and Geneva took him in. But Cyrus was a character, you never knew from one day to the next what was really going on with him. Just when Monique thought she had him figured out he would do something to question his choices in life. They were cool though, he was her confidant and she his, and there were times their relationship was rocky, but they managed to get through it. They were family and at the end of the day that meant something to her.

"To rest for a couple of days. That's all. I slept a lot last night and today, so I feel better."

Redemptive

"What do you need me to do, while I'm here?" asked Geneva between taking bites of food from her plate. "Nothing. I'm good."

"Now I don't mind, Monique. It's got to be something you need done." Looking around the room, Geneva was trying to find anything that needed attention in her opinion. She wouldn't find anything. Monique had a cleaning service that came every week to manage the upkeep of the house. Since she and Amar worked ridiculous hours, neither had time or the energy to do much cleaning and hiring someone was best for them. So there really wasn't anything for Geneva to do. Besides, Monique didn't want her snooping around in her things. It would give her more ammunition to talk about.

Amar was in the kitchen loading the dishwasher half listening to the conversation going on in the den when Monique got his attention.

"Isn't it TIME for me to take my medication?" Trying to be subtle in letting him know their time was up. The visit had gone well for the most part, but before it got out of hand she wanted to go head and cut it.

"I believe it is time," he said picking up on her subtle hint.

"Well, thank you for coming to check on me. I'm good. But I need to take my meds and follow the doctor's orders and get some rest."

Not waiting for them to respond, Monique stood up to walk them to the door. Getting the hint, they both stood and followed her. They thanked Amar for the food on the way out and told Monique they would call her the next day. She didn't hesitate to close the door behind them. On a good day she might have waited for them to reach the car, but not today. She wasn't in the mood for visitors and she wanted time alone with Amar.

"You did good, I'm proud of you," Amar told her when she came from the foyer. Monique didn't say anything just shrugged her shoulders.

"I'll be through with the dishes in a minute and we can talk about your dream."

A knot rose in the pit of Monique's stomach at those words. How could she have suppressed something so detrimental for so many years? Why now? Was it because she hit her head that jarred the memory? She

Redemptive

didn't know. Each step to the bedroom became harder and harder to take. Feeling like lead was suddenly in her shoes, she almost wished she hadn't said anything to Amar just yet. But it was out there now, and she'd have to deal with it.

Amar was rough around the edges, but he was also compassionate. Monique knew in her heart of hearts he would be there for her no matter what, but this was fresh, raw, and real. What she didn't need was for him to tell her to get over it. She would probably go off if he did. Or if he asked her questions she didn't have the answers to yet. *This is some deep stuff. This person is still alive, well known and living his life with his family. How am I going to handle this?* Many thoughts were running through her head when Amar came in with a beer.

"Where's mine?" asked Monique.

"Medication."

"Damn. That's right."

"Let's talk about this dream," said Amar as he swigged from the bottle of beer.

"It was a dream but not, more like a memory. When I was thirteen my cousin and I went to this summer camp. The youth pastor molested me one day in the cabin the first time, when I went back to get my notebook. The next time was in his office, when I was up there making copies for my group leader. One other time before camp was over, I took my cousin with me, but he sent him back to the group and it happened again." Crying as she remembered each encounter and reliving the shame all over again, Monique fell over on the bed. Amar took the last swig of his beer, got on the bed and held her in his arms.

"I'm sorry that happened to you Mon, but you survived it. You are the strongest woman I know. You haven't let it stop you from being you."

By the time she cried it out, her head was pounding, her eyes were swollen, and her mouth was dry.

"How do you want to handle it?" Amar asked after she finished crying.

"I don't know. I need some time to think about it. He is a big-time pastor now."

"The hell with that! That don't change the fact of what he did. Don't try to protect him if revealing it is what you need to do to heal from it. You decide and only you. I'm here with you either way."

Monique felt a huge weight fall from her shoulders. Amar's words made her feel better, but she still needed time. She got up, went to the bathroom and washed her face while Amar went to get water for her to take her meds.

Redemptive

That night Monique slept peacefully without one flash or thought about the molestation. She wasn't sure why, maybe she would never know, but the reality was alive and well in her consciousness now and she wouldn't let it go.

Chapter 6

Tension

A few days passed without Monique or Amar talking about the molestation. She felt better physically and against Amar's wishes, returned to work. The lump on her head was gone now and she hadn't had a headache or a dream in several days. Monique couldn't stand being idle so going to work was a no brainer for her. When she woke that morning and started to get dressed, Amar wanted to know where she was going.

"I'm going to work, where else would I be going this time of morning?" Standing in front of the mirror combing her hair, Monique didn't miss a beat.

"Today is Friday and I think you should rest this one last day," Amar said as he made the bed.

Redemptive

"No, I've rested enough and I'm going to work." Putting the comb on the tray that sat on top of her dresser, Monique turned to find Amar shaking his head. Refusing to start an argument so early in the morning, she grabbed her work bag and headed for the kitchen. The coffee was ready, so she grabbed two cups and filled them. Amar made his way to the kitchen picking up his cup and thanking her for pouring it.

"What do you want for breakfast," he asked. Monique could tell by his tone he was upset with her.

"Why don't we grab something on the way in?" asking while drinking from her cup hoping he would buy into that idea.

She knew the look too well. When he didn't agree with something he would give her a look without saying one word. She'd seen it twice this morning so far. All Monique wanted to do was get out of the house and go to work. It was too early in the morning for such attitude.

"An egg and bacon sandwich," was all she would say after his non-responsive answer.

"Fine."

Monique turned on the TV to check the weather and listen to the morning news. She wasn't exactly sure what was going on with Amar, it had to be more than her returning to work. Knowing she couldn't push the issue with him, she would have to wait until he was ready to talk to her about it.

By the time she'd heard the weather and the headline news, Amar had her sandwich ready. Trying to lighten the mood, she asked about the weekend.

Amar managed to keep the rest of the family at bay, but the weekend was coming and they hadn't seen or talked to Monique in a week. The house would be flooded with family over the weekend and they both knew it. Their house was the gathering place and they didn't really mind having people over but sometimes it was a bit too much. They loved entertaining, minus the drama, which somebody always manage to bring in some form. Amar was already preparing a menu and had discussed it with her briefly. One thing Monique never worried about was eating. Amar always made sure they ate well. The family may not have cared for him, but they never turned down an opportunity to be recipients of his blessings.

Monique and Amar were hard workers. Most days they spent ten or twelve hours at work depending on the workload. The business was doing well so it didn't leave much time for anything else. Occasionally they managed a long weekend here or there, but mostly

Redemptive

worked. Monique took way more time off than Amar, usually with her friend Sam who was her ride or die chick. The two had been friends for years and knew each other's secrets well and would take them to their graves. Sometimes Monique would take Shane and Tychia, along with her daughter Camille.

"Do I get to drive you into work, or don't I have a say in that either?" Amar asked while wiping down the counter but paused to wait for her answer.

Monique was starting to get pissed off with this attitude but refused to buy into whatever was going on with him. Taking a long deep breath before answering and looking him square in the face said, "Of course I am riding with you, do you think I should be driving yet?

The two gathered their things and drove to work in silence. Listening to music from the radio was the only form of communication between them.

Chapter 7

Amar

Friday night Amar stayed up late seasoning chicken and chopping potatoes for the potato salad. Monique offered to help but he insisted she rest. The weekend was probably going to be too much for her so rest was probably a good idea. She hadn't put up too much of a fuss since Amar had been distant.

Listening to smooth jazz, occasionally sipping a Corona, Amar continued to prep the food for the next day. He thought about Monique and how much he loved her, never wanted anything to happen to her, so part of him felt he failed her from the attacker. He was still waiting to hear back from the president of the neighborhood watch regarding more patrol in the neighborhood. Surely they were paying enough in dues to have added protection. He wasn't just

Redemptive

concerned for Monique but for everyone who lived there. He also thought about the dreams Monique was having and the realization of being molested. All he wanted was for her to be happy. Within a week, her happiness had been shattered and he just wanted to somehow fix it. If he could find the SOB who attacked her, that would solve one problem, but the second problem, Monique would have to decide how she wanted to handle that one. Trying to give her space, to decide how she wanted to pursue the issue was taking too long in his mind. He had his ideas, but it had to be her way. He would have to be patient, but it wasn't easy.

Grabbing the Corona from the counter, he took a long swig from the bottle. When he was finished he slammed the bottle back on the counter cracking it. Thankfully it didn't break or shatter, that was the last thing he needed right now. Putting the bottle in the trash and making sure no remnants were left behind Amar took another from the fridge. This time he was more careful of his placement of the bottle on the counter. Resuming his chopping and dicing, he tuned into the music and a song by Frankie Beverly was playing. He smiled at the thought of he and Mon dancing and the fun times they had together. Their life had been good. Totally different than his past and he was glad they'd met.

Amar's background had been somewhat shady, but always manage to make a good living. Family was important to him and he never had a problem taking care of them. When his wife stood by him when he served time in prison, he knew he would always be obligated to her. He was still honoring that obligation and would continue to do it. But then he met Monique. Feisty, vibrant, and full of life she awakened something in him that had been dead for a long time. When the two began spending more and more time together Amar knew he couldn't walk away from what they were building.

In his Muslim faith, a man can have more than one wife as long as one knows about the other. His dilemma was convincing the two women to agree to it because it went against the rules if they didn't.

His life with Paulina, the first wife was simple. They lived in separate states even before Monique came in the picture. Their arrangement worked for many years and it wasn't a big deal when he and Monique started dating. He never hid anything from Monique, so she was aware of his situation from the beginning.

Redemptive

Another rule of having multiple wives was they had to be treated equally. One wife could not possess or receive more than the other wife or wives. Amar made sure both women were provided for without question. Monique never wanted to be tied down to any relationship for long and so when he approached her with the proposition, she willingly agreed. He loved both women but in very different ways.

Before long Amar finished his prep work, put the food in the refrigerator in the garage, cleaned the kitchen and headed to bed. He was surprised when he entered the bedroom to find Monique awake.

"Why you up? Did you have another dream?" he asked while preparing to shower.

"No, I was asleep for a while but just woke up."

"Do you need something before I get in the shower?"

"No, I'm good."

Monique watched Amar gather his things. She didn't understand the distance but knew he wouldn't talk about what was bothering him until he was ready. Before he went into the bathroom he kissed her on the forehead and then took his shower.

"That was weird," she said after he went into the bathroom.

Chapter 8

The Family

The phone rang bright and early Saturday morning. Monique grabbed it after she heard Amar groan from the noise. Taking the phone from the cradle she went toward the den.

"Hello," she said in almost a whisper.

"Mon, what time should I come over today. Girl we got so much to talk about."

"Why is you calling my house this early in the morning Cyrus? The day ain't going nowhere." Shaking her head at the foolishness early in the morning, Monique walked to the kitchen to pour a cup of coffee. Amar must have forgot to set the timer last night, because there was no coffee. Now she had to listen to Cyrus without any caffeine.

Redemptive

"I think I will drive out around twelve. That should give you and Amar time to get yourself together and fire up the grill."

"See that's what I'm talking about right there. Why is you planning someone else's day? Why don't you let me call you back when I get myself together." Before Cyrus could say anything else, Monique hung up the phone and placed it on the bar. Walking around to the other side she turned on the coffee maker and pulled down two mugs. She knew it would be a matter of time before Amar was up moving around. She also knew it wouldn't be long before the next call.

True to form the phone rang before the coffee could finish dripping. This time looking at the caller ID, it was her son Shane.

"Hey son."

"Hey Ma. How you feeling?"

"Much better. I went back to work yesterday."

"Amar was good with that?"

"No but I went anyway."

"What ya'll got going on today? Me and the fam was thinking bout coming through."

"Nothing. I think Amar might be throwing something on the grill later."

"Aiight, we'll see you later."

"Bye."

Monique poured the coffee in the mugs and met Amar in the hall when she started back to the bedroom. She handed him his mug and he kissed her good morning.

"Who was that calling here so damn early in the morning?" he asked.

"Take one guess."

"Cyrus needs to get a life. He's got way too much time on his hands."

"Don't I know it."

"What time is the cleaning crew coming today?"

Looking at the clock at the end of the hall she realized they should be there soon. "Nine."

"That's in thirty minutes. What do you want for breakfast?"

"Let's just run around the corner and grab something, since we don't have a lot of time."

Redemptive

"Okay. Go throw something on and let's go." Without hesitation, Monique started toward the bathroom, surprised at how Amar agreed so easily to eating out.

The two washed their faces, brushed their teeth and headed to the mom and pop diner around the corner. They ordered two breakfast specials and made it back just in time for the cleaners.

#####

The phone continued to rang constantly throughout the morning just as Monique and Amar expected. Before the morning was over the family had all made plans to spend the day at their house.

"Did you get a chance to do your morning prayers?"

"Yes."

Back to the one-word answers Monique thought to herself. Not one to bite her tongue, she was trying to be patient with him, but he was starting to get on her nerves with the lack of communication. *Just say what's on your mind already and let's move on.* Again, another thought running through her head.

#####

By noon the doorbell started to ring. Cyrus and Geneva were standing at the door looking like cats that ate the canary. Monique let them in while wondering what they were up to now. Sometimes she really wondered about the two of them, but then again they only traveled like that when they were about to be messy.

The day turned out to be sunny and gorgeous with low humidity. It was perfect for the family to sit outside on the back-patio Amar had built. Extending from the existing patio, a large pad was poured for an outdoor oasis. The covered patio housed a kitchen area, ample seating room, a fireplace, and a bar. The overhead lighting allowed for late night entertaining. Patio furniture was placed throughout the space for grouped conversations. What everybody loved was the half brick walls that felt like they were in another room off to itself.

"Where's Amar?" Cyrus asked looking around.

"Outback," Monique replied. You can go out there, he's getting ready to fire up the grill."

"Naw, I'm good."

"Let's not start that today Cyrus. We all are going out there eventually. At some point in time you are going to have to see him." Monique could feel the agitation already starting to stir in her. *Not even in the house five*

Redemptive

minutes and the drama was already starting. *Why come to the house if you don't want to acknowledge the man of the house,* she thought? *Dumb....just plain dumb.*

"I'm just not ready to go out there yet. You know I'm gonna go Mon so don't trip."

Looking at her cousin Monique could only wonder what he and Geneva talked about in the car ride over. She was unusually quiet today. *Don't go borrowing trouble,* Monique told herself. Moving through the kitchen Monique called Amar on the intercom. "What do you want me to bring out next?"

"You can bring the potato salad, some of the beer that's in the pantry, to go in the fridge out here. Also bring dish towels."

"Okay, I'll be right out." Gathering the things together, Monique didn't look at her mother or cousin, knowing they were eying her. When Monique headed toward the back door, the doorbell rang. "Could one of you get the door?" she asked while walking out the backdoor.

Monique nudged Amar when she got out back. "Cyrus and Geneva are here, and the doorbell just rang, I'm not sure who it is, but I'll say it's about to be on."

Amar laughed, brushing the last bit of sauce on the chicken. "With your family it always is."

More and more people continued to show up. Before long the family had gathered, the food and drinks were flowing, and the music was in full effect. From the youngest to the oldest, they laughed, danced and drank. Things were going well until Geneva got started, interrupting the flow of everything.

"Well Monique, everybody is waiting to hear from you what happened and how you feeling now."

Geneva knew how Monique felt about being put on the spot like that but insisted on doing it anyway. With all attention on Monique, her first thought was to give Geneva a few choice words, but she was really trying lately to work on her relationship with the Lord, so she decided against it.

"Thank y'all for your concern, but I'm fine as you can see. The doctor told me to rest for a few days and I did." Monique was glad to be finished with her meds because right now all she wanted was to drink from her bottle of Corona and be done. Turning to go somewhere, anywhere than being the center of attention, Geneva's words stopped her in her tracks.

"But Monique you didn't tell them what happened. They want to hear the story. You can't just walk off like that."

Redemptive

Now Monique was mad. Why does she always have to go too far? Don't know how to leave well enough alone. Just gotta have that extra push. Okay, I'll fix her, she thought.

"How many of y'all already heard the story from Geneva or Cyrus, raise your hand? Come on, I know one of them called you and told you what happened."

One by one, hands started going up. Looking at Geneva Monique simply said, "I'm sure you did a good job in telling them. I don't need to repeat it." Without another word Monique walked in the house. Hearing the clacking of heels behind her, Monique knew Tychia was getting ready to get on her nerves next. When she suddenly stopped, Tychia almost bumped into her.

"What do you need Ty?" Monique asked in her already frustrated state.

"Moni, can we not fight today? Everybody came here to see you."

Walking around to the kitchen to sit at the bar, Monique looked at her daughter in law with furled brows. "What *we* Ty? And who's fighting? I said what I had to say and I'm done."

"But Moni"……..before she could finish, Monique's Aunt Sylvia walked in.

"Monique stop letting your mama get under your skin like that. You know how she is, this ain't about her today. Come on back outside so we can enjoy you. That's what we're here for."

Monique loved her Aunt Sylvia and the two were extremely close. She admired her wisdom and her ability above all else to keep her calm. Knowing her aunt was right, but Monique wanted to stew just a bit longer.

"Come on now, daylight ain't gone hold for long and I need to be able to see how to get out of here before it gets too late."

The women laughed and Monique along with Aunt Sylvia and Ty went to rejoin the others. When they got back outside a group had just formed a line for the Cupid shuffle and the three women jumped right in. The laughter returned while Monique focused on her dance moves. Looking over at Amar at one point, he winked at her and raised his beer in approval. After the song ended, Monique avoided her mother as much as she could. Between crying babies, card games, folk telling lies, eating, drinking and dancing, it wasn't hard to do. She did manage to have short

Redemptive

conversations with a couple of her other aunts, a couple of her nieces and of course her kids. Shane and Camille got a chance to have alone time with her at the end of the night when almost everyone was gone. Sitting around the outdoor fireplace, the three started out making small talk about the day. Before long the conversation quickly got serious.

"Ma do you think they will catch the dude that did this to you?" Shane asked, his voice showing concern.

"I don't know son. It's hard to say, but Amar reported it to the president of the Neighborhood watch, and they are beefing up security. They are also making everyone aware throughout the neighborhood."

"I wouldn't have thought anything like that would happen out here," Camille said while leaning against Monique's arm."

"Don't worry yourself about this. It's over and I'm not worried about the guy coming back. If he does I have something for him."

Camille and Shane both laughed at her knowing without any doubt, she could take care of herself. Looking around the backyard patio, Monique turned to Shane and asked where was his wife.

"I don't know, probably in the house watching TV."

"Why, when it's a TV out here. Camille, go see where Ty is and tell her to come out here with us."

Without hesitation Camille went to look for her sister in law. Shane and Monique exchanged looks but neither said a word. Monique knew Ty's reputation and although she loved her daughter in law, let's just say for now she had a problem with her being alone in her house. The moment was tense but didn't last long when Camille's daughter Candace came crying to Monique about one of the other children not playing fair. Taking time to console the crying child took their attention to something else.

Before long Camille and Ty came out and joined the others laughing looking like they were both half high and everything was fine. Monique told them on several occasion not to be smoking in her house. She didn't call them out on it but gave a disapproving look. They both knew she would deal with that later. Shane got up to help Amar clean up what was left of the food and the outdoor kitchen area to avoid any confrontation that may ensue between the women.

####

Later that night when the house was empty Amar and Monique lay in bed talking about the day. There was something about the darkness that made Amar want

Redemptive

to open up and talk. Monique didn't question it, she just rolled with it.

"Overall I think it was a good day Mon," he said in a low tone. Monique could hear the tiredness in his voice.

"Except for Geneva and her mess, I think it went okay."

"Yeah, she could have kept that."

"For real. Did you see Ty roaming around in the house today?"

"No. Why, is something missing?"

Monique was glad for the darkness because Amar couldn't see her face when she smiled. They knew her too well and the trouble she'd brought to the family over the years, not to mention the things that mysteriously disappeared!

"I don't know. She lingered in the house too long for my comfort. I sent Camille in to get her. I wasn't sure if you saw her or not."

"No, I didn't, but I guess we'll find out soon enough."

Chapter 9

Camille

Camille was Monique's youngest child. She was raising two children on her own and overall was doing well with it. Monique admired her daughter's hustle to work and provide for her children. The father was absentee in the children's lives despite how he managed to do everything else but be there. An able-bodied young man who hadn't found his purpose in life as of yet, lacked the skills to be a father. So Camille had moved on.

Camille's job as a program manager for a data company afforded her a decent lifestyle. Although it would have been nice to have financial support from the children's father, their lives worked well without it. She was confident, focused, and had goals for what she wanted in life. Her job required her to work hard, but she played just as hard. Sometimes Monique

Redemptive

worried whether or not the smoking and drinking was a bit too much, but hey she was grown, so she trusted Camille to handle her business.

Nothing came before Cameron and Candace though, Camille made sure of that. Everyone had to admit Candace was a bit spoiled and at four years old hadn't grown out of her whiny phase. It was hard for anyone to babysit for that very reason, but occasionally Camille would get someone in the family to agree. Cameron was six years older and more responsible for his age. His grades were good, and he was becoming a respectable young man.

Camille and Shane's relationship was close. The two spent a lot of time together talking or texting about life, the family, or anything else they could think of. Shane worked a lot so they couldn't see each other as much as she liked. Camille loved her brother very much. She even liked her sister in law Tychia but didn't like some of the things she did. Ty came from a good family, but something was broken in her. Camille couldn't get with the whole being extra, wanting more than what she had or anybody else for that matter and it made her time hanging with her short.

When she wanted to see her brother though, Shane tried to make himself available and Ty never hindered her from doing so. Shane and Ty decided not to have children, so Camille didn't have anyone to spoil but her own children.

######

Camille called Monique one day in a panic. When Monique answered the phone, Camille was distraught. "What is it?" Monique asked after hearing her daughter's voice.

"Is Amar home?" Camille asked heaving through her words.

"No. This is his weekend to be away."

"I'm coming out there, I need to tell you something."

"No, Camille, you sound too upset to drive, let me come to you. I'll be there within the hour."

"Okay."

Monique hung up the phone, puzzled about Camille's call. She was always strong and together, but this was so out of character for her. Slipping on her shoes and making sure all the doors were locked, Monique got in her car and drove to Camille's house. The ride seemed longer than usual while Monique maneuvered through evening traffic she replayed the call over and over in her mind. What in the name of all things holy could this be? she asked herself. The poor baby

Redemptive

sounded like her world just came to an end. Gripping the steering wheel as she drove, Monique took deep breaths to slow her pounding heart from jumping out of her chest. When she finally pulled into the driveway and shut off the engine, Camille was standing in the doorway. Monique made her way to her daughter as fast as she could and held her in her arms. Not wanting to be rude or insensitive, Monique pulled away from her and suggested they get inside. Closing the door behind her they sat in the family room.

"What's going on?" Monique questioned her visibly shaken daughter.

"I went to use one of my credit cards today and it was declined."

Trying her best to remain calm, Monique waited for Camille to finish talking because this couldn't be why she was so upset. "Did you use another card?"

"You don't understand. I've only used that card once and I only spent fifty dollars."

"Camille, that's not enough for you to be so upset. What's going on? Did you cancel the card?"

Nodding her head yes, Camille blew her nose and before continuing, sighed. "When they faxed me over the documents from the transactions I recognized the handwriting."

"Who's handwriting is it?" Monique's heartbeat was racing once again while she waited for her daughter to say the one name she didn't want to hear.

Chapter 10

Cyrus

While Monique drove home that night her head was spinning from the words Camille told her. Not again she told herself. They couldn't go through this again. When was this going to stop? The phone rang and Monique saw it was Cyrus.

"Hey Cyrus."

"Moni, hey. We didn't get a chance to talk the weekend, it was just too much going on, so I thought I'd call and catch you up on what's going on."

"It's not really a good time right now, Cyrus."

"Why? You with Amar?"

"No Cyrus, it's just not a good time."

"Moni, you shouldn't be like that. Ever since your attack you haven't been the same. I know you went through something, but you've just been different."

"Oh boy, here we go. What's so important Cyrus that you have to tell me right now or you gone bust a gut?"

Totally disregarding her comment, Cyrus went into his spiel. "I was talking to Geneva and Moni she don't understand why you are so upset with her? I tried to explain it to her the best I could but she ain't getting it."

Trying her best not to go off with this foolishness once again, Monique took a second before answering him.

"Cyrus why do you feel the need to run interference with me and Geneva? Geneva know she messy and you trying to clean it up ain't helping. I got too much going on in my life right now to fool with you or Geneva."

"Well hell, I'm just trying to help. You can be short Moni and people take that the wrong way sometimes. If you explain……..

Monique cut him off before he finished his sentence. "Wait a minute Cyrus, what you ain't fidna do is tell me how to handle Geneva. I didn't ask for your help and I don't need it."

Redemptive

"All I'm sayin"…….

"You've said enough for tonight. I'm trying to get home, I got a headache already and you ain't helping it."

"One more thing before you get off the phone. I mean, I ain't really had a chance to talk to you lately.

"What is it Cyrus, just spit it out already!"

"Can I hold a hundred until I get paid next week?"

"Are you gone pay me the last hundred you borrowed last week too?"

"See there you go Moni! Why you got to bring that up now? I just asked you a simple question."

"And I asked you one. You want me to keep giving you money when you haven't paid back the money you owe me. I am not your personal banker, Cyrus." Pissed off royally now, Monique was trying to remain true to her promise of not cussing people out since she really was trying to get closer to the Lord.

"Forget I asked," Cyrus said only out of frustration.

"Forgotten."

Chapter 11

Monique and Cyrus

Monique didn't like the way her conversation ended with Cyrus. Things had been tense between them and she didn't like it. Despite his issues and needing to get his life together, they were close. They held the other's secrets and had gotten through rough times together over the years. He was like a brother to her and she didn't want that to change but she also needed to set boundaries about money. She was tired of being the financial crutch for everyone else's needs and it was time to put a stop to it.

Since it was Amar's weekend to be away, it was the perfect time for the two to get together. After her morning walk through the neighborhood, choosing not to use the trail again yet, she showered and called Cyrus.

Redemptive

"Hey," she said when he answered.

"Hey," he replied, but was a bit short.

"I was thinking since Amar is gone this weekend, maybe we could get lunch and hang out a bit."

Monique waited for his response, knowing he was being deliberate in answering as a way of punishing her.

"Sure, where you wanna go?"

"Let's ride to Dane's."

"What time?"

"Can you be ready in an hour?"

"Yeah, see you then."

When Monique hung up she couldn't help but laugh at Cyrus and the games he liked to play. Maybe one day he will grow up but she wouldn't hold her breath for that one. After straightening a few things in the house and making her bed, Monique grabbed her keys and headed to Cyrus' place.

The warmth of the sun caused the chill in the air to disappear and Monique opened the sunroof to her SUV to take in the fresh air. Traffic was minimal so it didn't take her long to get to the city. To her surprise Cyrus was ready and waiting for her when she arrived.

"What's up Mon?" getting in the truck and throwing his bag in the back.

"What's goin on?" she said, pulling out of the driveway and heading toward the interstate.

The two made small talk in the beginning. They talked about their week, a silly show on TV and the gathering at Monique's house. Suddenly the climate changed in the conversation.

"Monique, do you think you can give Aunt Geneva a break? It's obvious to the family how you are treating her and people are talking."

"Cyrus, when have I ever cared about what people think? Just know I have my reasons and they keep growing by the minute."

"I'm just say…….."

"You always just saying something Cyrus. You shouldn't defend things you know nothing about."

"What don't I know Moni?"

By now Cyrus turned in the seat facing Monique. Monique kept her eyes on the road as if she didn't

Redemptive

notice the gesture. Waiting like a child expecting a treat, he stared at her waiting for a response.

"Why is you looking at me like you crazy?"

"I'm waiting on you to answer me. You've avoided that question for too long, but not today Mon. I wanna know what this rift is, and it goes deeper than her being a busybody."

"Can we pause this? I planned to talk to you about this today as a matter of fact, but I don't want to get into it while I'm driving. I promise when we get to the restaurant I will answer that question. I just hope you ready for the answer."

"Aiight Moni, but don't think you are getting out of this."

Cyrus repositioned himself in the seat so he was no longer staring at Monique. The two rode for a few minutes in complete silence, which Monique welcomed to change the mood of such a heavy conversation.

"Oh, what have you been on your head to tell me? I mean you made it sound like the world was gone come to an end if you didn't tell me."

"So I've been thinking about a change."

"What kind of change?" Monique gave him the side eye waiting for the foolishness about to come out of his mouth.

"Well you know how I've been kinda struggling lately so I think I may try somewhere new. I was talking to Aunt Geneva about it and she thinks it's a good idea."

"First of all, you a grown ass man, why do you need anybody's approval to do what you already know you want to do? Secondly, I think it's dumb for you to leave. Where you going? What's your plan?"

"I'm working on it Mon, damn! All I said was I was thinking about it."

"You can't get your life together cause you let everything else come before your responsibilities. You too old to be always starting over Cyrus. Take a year, cut out the extra crap you got going on and see where your life will be then. If you still feel like you need a new start, at least it will give you time to plan for one. But jumping from here to there ain't gone fix that."

"Well I guess you told me, huh?"

"Ain't you tired of this rollercoaster of a life you got? Hell, I'm tired of it for you."

Quietness fell between the two again. This time they would be close to their destination before anyone

Redemptive

spoke another word. When they arrived at Dane's the wait wasn't as long as Monique had anticipated. While she and Cyrus waited, their people watching caused them to talk to each other again after a few laughs at the expense of others. The fashion statements alone was enough for them to look at each other without saying a word. They were in a college town on a Saturday afternoon and it was obvious by the way most were dressed.

After about a forty-five-minute wait, Monique and Cyrus were called to be seated. It didn't take either one long to order since they had time to decide. When the waitress left, Cyrus leaned back in his seat waiting for Monique to resume their conversation from the ride up. Looking at the way he watched her Monique thought something really had to be wrong with him. What man was so eager to hear any form of gossip, but Cyrus wasn't any man. Amar would never hound her for information like this. He would be like, whatever Mon, and go on with his life. But not Cyrus with his nosey self. Deciding not to delay this story any longer, she leaned forward to tell Cyrus what he so desperately wanted to know.

"Well let me start out by saying I just recently recalled the details of what I'm about to tell you. I haven't had this conversation with anyone else but Amar."

"Okay."

"When I was attacked and hit my head, it jogged a memory, I guess I buried years ago. Remember when Geneva used to send us to church camp for the summer and after a while we hated going?"

Cyrus' whole demeanor changed when Monique asked the question but didn't understand why. Her immediate thought was Cyrus was just being his normal dramatic self. Ignoring the blank look on his face, she went on with the story.

"Well I don't know if you all had much interaction with Pastor Daniels, but he spent a lot of time over on our side and he molested me three times. The last time I tried to take Sam with me but he sent her back to where the others were, making us be alone in his office. I just wonder how many other girls he did that to. I couldn't have been the only one."

Cyrus sat frozen. Monique was surprised because she expected a different reaction from him. The noise in the restaurant was high, so Monique tried to keep the level of her voice just loud enough for only her and Cyrus to hear what she was saying. Still waiting for Cyrus to respond, Monique finally asked what was wrong with him.

Redemptive

"What are you planning on doing about this now that you remember?" asked Cyrus, looking concerned.

"That's all you got to say?" Monique still didn't get his behavior.

"I think you should leave this alone, Mon, it was a long time ago."

"Wait a minute. What's up with this? I'm sitting here telling you what happened to me and the trauma of it all and all you can say is leave it alone? And what the hell does time have to do with it Cyrus?"

Her anger was rising now, and Monique couldn't help but think this reaction would be exactly how Geneva would react and it made the anger worse. Cyrus was never without a dramatic reaction to anything, so this was totally out of character.

"Excuse me Mon, I'm going to the bathroom." Before Monique could say anything Cyrus had gotten up from their booth and headed to the bathroom.

Monique sat confused. "Did I say something to offend him?" she asked herself. "How did I offend him by what I said?" It was the strangest thing. What am I missing? A few minutes later Cyrus returned.

"Do you mind if we take our food to go?"

"No, we drove an hour and a half we are not taking any food to go. Sit down! Besides, we are suppose to make a day out of it. What's going on Cyrus? Why are you acting like this? Talk to me. What is it?"

"That man molested me Mon, over and over again."

Completely shocked by this news, Monique fell back in her seat. Looking at her cousin now all she could see was the innocent boy he was when he came to live with them when his mother died.

"What the hell?" she said when she finally managed to speak. "Why didn't you tell me?"

"What was I suppose to say Mon?"

"I don't know," she whispered with her head now bowed. "It was so traumatic you see I am only remembering thirty something years later and it took a bump on the head to trigger that. That nasty SOB!!! We have to do something about it."

"No! I can't. I'm not strong like you Mon. Do you know how powerful he is now?"

"I don't give a damn about that Cyrus. It's gotta be more out there……..

Before Monique could finish Cyrus stopped her mid-sentence.

Redemptive

"I can't. I just can't." Visibly shaken by the thought of it all, Cyrus was pleading with Monique.

"Don't you think if you confront this, the sooner you and I can get on with our lives and not have this haunting us? You know I always wondered why I was the way I was toward men; my way or the highway, my rules or else. I am now starting to understand where all that stems from."

"You've always been the bully Mon, but I just can't do it. I can't, I can't, I can't." Cyrus was getting louder and Monique felt he was about to make a scene.

"Okay, okay, just calm down. People are starting to stare over here. I think we need to take this to go after all."

When they got back in the truck Cyrus asked Monique again what she planned to do.

"I don't know yet, but know I'm not fidna let this go. That I won't do, not after what you just told me."

Chapter 12

Monique

Days after Monique and Cyrus took their road trip she agonized over how she would handle this mess with Pastor Daniels. The beloved Pastor Daniels, nothing but the devil in disguise. He was one of the reasons she hadn't wanted anything to do with the church for years.

She'd told Amar about her conversation with Cyrus when he got back in town from his weekend with Paulina. He had given her the same look she'd given Cyrus when he'd told her. Utterly disgusted already that he'd molested her and God knows how many other girls, only to find out he was molesting boys too, was too much for anyone to handle. It explained so much pertaining to Cyrus' struggles with his choices in life.

Redemptive

"That's some messed up shit right there," Amar told Monique when he heard the rest of the story. "What are you gonna do?" asking while sitting on the bed taking off his shoes.

"I don't know yet," she said, changing into her night gown. I've been thinking of doing something I never thought I would."

Turning around to face her with a puzzled look on his face, Amar waited for her to finish.

"Nothing like that," she assured him. "I'm thinking about seeing a counselor, just for a couple of sessions to kinda help me put some things in perspective."

"If that's what you want to do, I'll support you. Whatever it takes for you to be free of this shit."

"Thanks. Let's keep it between us for now."

"Who the hell I'm gone tell? Your crazy family?......they need to go with you. Maybe you can get a family discount." Amar chuckled as he said the last part. Monique couldn't help but laugh at the idea herself.

"I'm just sayin and yes we all need to be in there, but you can't talk with the shit you got going on in your own life."

"At least I know mine is what it is, y'all don't know it yet."

"Good night Amar, glad you made it back safe."

"Good night Mon."

####

The next morning as Monique and Amar was getting ready for work, the phone rang and it was Geneva. Monique ignored the call. Gathering the last of her things Monique met Amar in the car and they headed to work.

"Are you gone call Geneva?" asked Amar.

"No."

"You know she's gone keep calling."

"I know and I will keep ignoring until I'm ready to talk to her."

"Alright, I'll leave it alone."

"Thanks, appreciate it."

Monique got to work and started her day. Engrossed in the matters of the business she didn't realize it was

Redemptive

lunchtime until her assistant asked her what she wanted for lunch.

"I'm good, I brought lunch for me and Amar. Thanks though, she said.

She turned back to her desk and continued working. It wasn't long before Monique felt someone standing in her doorway. "Yes, can I help you?" she asked without looking up.

"You can start by taking my phone calls, so I don't have to drive over here to talk to you."

Monique paused at the sound of Geneva's voice. Turning around in her chair for the second time in as many minutes to see Geneva standing waiting for an invitation to enter.

"What are you doing here?" Monique asked, her agitation was obvious.

"Don't you listen Monique? I just said if you returned my phone calls, I wouldn't have to come over here."

"I'm working Geneva, so what's so important that you felt the need to drive over?"

"Cyrus called me all upset about you trying to destroy everybody's life."

"What the hell? Is that what Cyrus really said or is that you making shit up?"

"Well that's not exactly what he said, but that's the gist of it."

"I agree with Cyrus, Monique. That stuff happened a long time ago. You should just let it go. There is no need to mess up everybody's life hashing up old stuff. Besides why would you want to destroy Pastor Daniel's life? Everybody loves him.

"Are you serious right now? For real, for real….are you serious? If Cyrus told you everything and I'm sure he did, you know this man molested both of us and all you have to say is I shouldn't hash up old stuff. What kind of mama are you, Geneva? The best thing for you to do is leave my office before I say something to hurt your feelings."

"But Moni…………"

Before Geneva could finish, Monique cut her off.

"Go head Geneva, it's time for you to leave. I'm not talking about this with you here. I'm done with this conversation. I need to get back to work."

Turning back around to face her computer, Monique could hear the footsteps of Geneva going down the hall. Fuming from the gall of her coming to her

Redemptive

workplace to talk about this foolishness was a new low even for Geneva, especially suggesting that she let it go. It would be a cold day in hell before that ever happened.

Chapter 13

Counseling

Dr. Regina Meyers was the counselor Monique chose from a list of internet recommendations. It was something that spoke to her spirit when she read her bio and reviews from satisfied clients. Even the less than five-star reviews were not really bad reviews. When she'd made the call, an appointment was available within a couple of days.

Monique wasn't sure what to expect when she first entered Dr. Meyers office, but it wasn't long before she felt comfortable and at ease with the approach the doctor used. It was more conversational than clinical, although Monique knew the doctor was taking notes.

As the weeks progressed on, she opened up more. The sessions started to move beyond the molestation and

Redemptive

Monique was able to talk about other issues in her life. After each session she left feeling less burdened and freer. It was invigorating to talk to someone where you were not always having to defend the conversation. Dr. Meyers was helping her see for the first time in her life that she didn't have to be bound by her past or carry the weight of other people's issues. She wasn't their savior and it was time for her to give up that role. But it was an area in her life in which she struggled. Monique loved her family very much, despite their issues. Hell, she had her own, but the toxicity of their lives was taking a toll on her more than she realized, and it was time for her to break that cycle.

The sessions also helped her with her relationship with Amar. Overall their marriage was good, and it was working. Monique didn't have a problem with him being gone twice a month to be with Paulina, it was a welcomed time for her. Most people would never agree to be a part of such a triangle. It was an unusual situation and she knew the family talked about it, but didn't care. It was her choice and she'd made no apologies for it. Besides, she and Amar were smart about planning. Provisions had been made to take care of her in the event of his death, so as far as "issues" were concerned, there were none. The counselor agreed that if it was working for the two of them, they should continue with their arrangement. But she did offer some different strategies in communication and behavior regarding him. Dr. Meyers was working with her on the defensive, 'let me get you before you get me', mindset. "It sounds like Amar is safe," she'd said, so that's not a battle you need to fight anymore.

Monique was trying to take those words to heart, so each day she would try more and more to be less defensive and more loving. This was new for her. It would take time and work to be comfortable in this new space.

One of the goals Monique and Dr. Meyers set was for her to face her abuser. They would take baby steps in planning the time and approach, but that would come at a later date. Monique was resistant in the beginning to wait, however listening to the advice of Dr. Meyers helped her see the importance of waiting.

Counseling was one of the best decisions Monique made in a very long time. One of the things she was putting to practice was to spend more time with Amar. Normally, her weekends were spent running around the city with any and everybody just to be busy. The first couple of weekends at home, made her realize, it wasn't just for Amar but for herself as well. Physically she was tired, mentally she was healing, spiritually she

Redemptive

was growing, and emotionally she was finding her balance.

One weekend when Monique and Amar was sitting out on the back patio having a drink while grilling steaks and listening to music, Amar told her how glad he was that she was home. Taken by surprise when he said it, her first reaction was to fire back with a smart remark, but she thought about what Dr. Meyers said and so she sat for a moment staring at him. For the first time Amar looked different to her, maybe it wasn't anything new about him, but about her, that made her feel that way. Without saying a word, she got up, walked over to the grill where he was standing and put her arms around his waist. This was a new move for her. She felt him pause, but then he turned toward her, kissed her passionately and the two danced to the sound of Luther playing in the background. That night they ate burnt steaks.

Chapter 14

A Visit with Grandma

With a busy work schedule, counseling sessions and taking care of Amar, Monique hadn't visited her Grandma in several weeks. It was totally out of character for her. She'd called her every week, but it wasn't the same as their visits together. Monique loved her grandma and they talked about everything. Before seeing Dr. Meyers, Grandma had been her voice of reason, her confidant, her best friend.

It was time for Amar to take his weekend trip and Monique would spend the day with Grandma. When Monique arrived, Grandma had cooked her favorite fried chicken, green beans, potato salad and candied yams. She'd picked up fresh strawberries from the market and made homemade cream to finish off the pound cake she baked.

Redemptive

The two women sat and ate together making small talk. Monique washed the dishes when they were finished, and the women went out on the porch enjoying the sunshine. The porch had an old swing, one of her uncles'-built years ago, so they headed toward it and begin slowly swinging.

"Geneva came by here last week all upset," her grandma said looking into the distance.

Rolling her eyes, Monique wasn't ready for this conversation. This was grandma so she wouldn't be disrespectful to her but would choose her words carefully in her response.

"What's going on with Geneva?"

"That's your mama, first off," her grandma scolded. Monique knew grandma was old school and didn't play when it came to things like manners and respect.

"Yes, grandma. What was she upset about?"

"I want this rift between the two of you to stop Monique. It's not healthy and at the end of the day she is your mama. You can't change that. She tells me bout you trying to bring down preacher Daniels. Is that true?"

Monique was trying to control her anger. See this was the problem she had with Geneva, only telling enough of any story to get mess started and she's off to the next thing. Taking a deep breath before she answered, Monique started from the beginning and told the entire story. When she finished, her grandma sat quietly, slowly rocking back and forth in the swing.

"I'm so sorry you went through that baby, I really am, but you need to let the good Lord fight this battle. It's not yours."

Looking at her grandma, Monique could not believe what she was hearing. This was the woman whom she admired most, the one she'd gone to for advice for most of her life. This couldn't be happening, not Grandma, please not her too.

"I'm sorry too Grandma, but I can't let it go. I don't know how many people have been affected by this man's filthy hands because I'd blocked it for so many years. If I can stop this I will. I don't know how yet, but I will in time."

"Lord, Monique, think about his family and the life he's built and the church he's built. Are you willing to destroy that? Can you live with yourself knowing that?"

"Grandma, are you saying to me that my life, and the lives of the other people he's molested don't matter? That's what I'm getting from this conversation. I don't

Redemptive

care about what he's built, his family or that damn church he stands in every Sunday and lie Sunday after Sunday."

"No, baby. I'm just saying let the Lord handle it."

"If the good Lord didn't want me to do something about it, He would have left it buried in my memory. I didn't hit my head and remembered this for nothing Grandma, I don't believe that."

"Lord, this is going to hurt so many people. It's gone be on the news and everything. Jesus I don't want to see him go down like that. It's so hard for a black man to have anything these days."

Monique was struggling with this conversation. "What the hell is Grandma thinking," she thought to herself.

"Well Grandma, he should have thought about that when his nasty behind was doing what he did in the name of the Lord. You just have to pray the Lord will get you through it, all of us for that matter."

"Don't sass me Monique. I won't tolerate that now."

"No Ma'am, I'm not sassing you Grandma, I'm just saying this isn't going to be easy for me to do but I believe I have to. Who knows how many other people will come forward, but somebody has to be the first one."

"God ain't sleep Monique. He knows all and sees all. He is the only one who can judge a person for their sins, not us."

"I'm not judging him, but I am going to confront him."

"Lord, have mercy."

####

Later that night when Monique arrived home, she showered and crawled in bed, flipping through the channels on the TV when the phone rang. It was Amar.

"Hey babe," he sounded excited to hear her voice when she answered.

Smiling when she heard his, she replied, "Hey."

"Whatchca up to?"

"Nothing much. Hadn't been too long getting home from Grandma's house."

"How'd did that go?"

"Not what I expected. The first part of the visit was good. She cooked. You know Grandma."

"Yeah, what'd she cook?"

"Fried chicken, green beans, and potato salad. She baked a pound cake, so we had strawberry shortcake."

Redemptive

"Sounds good. Tell me what happened," Amar sensing the tension in her voice.

"Geneva told her about the molestation, her version of it anyway and she doesn't want me to pursue it."

"Listen Mon, I know you love your grandma and you respect her opinion, but this has got to be your decision and nobody else."

"You're right Amar, it's just hard feeling like everybody is against you. That I am the only one willing to stand for what is right."

"You're not the only one, Mon. Your family is so used to covering things up and not dealing with hard issues. This is no different. But you can't continue to let them control your actions. This is yours to do with as YOU please, not them."

"Hey, is everything alright? I'm not use to getting a call from you."

"Yes, everything is fine. I just missed you that's all."

"Hey big man, I miss you too."

"Don't forget to turn the alarm on and I will see you on Monday. If you need me, call me."

"Okay. I will."

Chapter 15

The Drama Continues

Life had been hectic for Monique, so she hadn't talked to Camille or Shane to see what was going on in their worlds. It was even odd that Ty hadn't tried to reach out to her. She couldn't help but wonder what Camille decided to do about the stolen money, but one thing Monique was learning was to let people live their own lives. There was a time she had to admit when she would have been all up in the middle of that situation. She did miss them though and thought about having them out over the weekend. Just them, not the rest of the family. There needed to be distance between her and them for a minute.

Learning how to let go of things and not be so quick to react was starting to be her new normal and Monique was really enjoying it. She was liking the woman she was becoming, the possibilities of where life could take

Redemptive

her and she wasn't willing to compromise any of it, not for anyone.

One random Tuesday evening, Monique received a phone call from her ex-husband, Graham, the father of her children. The two remained friends after the divorce and both agreed they were better friends than they were husband and wife. Graham was a great provider and a great dad, but that's about where it ended especially toward the end of the marriage. He attended family functions and maintained a great relationship with the kids, so it wasn't really unusual to hear from him, but this was out of character even for him.

"Hey Graham, what's going on."

"Hey Mon, have you talked to Camille lately?"

"No. Is she okay?"

"She's really upset about this money thing and how she should handle it. I just thought you might need to talk to her about it."

"I thought she'd made a decision regarding it already. What is she waiting on?"

"She did with the credit card company, and they are doing their investigation, she's just trying to figure out whether or not to tell her brother."

"Well Graham, we've all known for a while, that girl has had a problem, even Shane. We all chose to look the other way. This is what happens when people don't deal with shit. It gets out of hand."

"Damn, what has happened to you? This doesn't sound like you."

"I'm trying to get my own life together. Part of it is not involving myself in other people's business."

"We're in it whether we want to be or not, Mon, that's real talk."

"I was thinking about having the kids out here over the weekend. I will see how things go and talk to Camille then. You are more than welcome to join us."

"I'll let you know. I'm suppose to go out of town for a job later in the week. I hope it brings me back by the weekend."

"Just let me know."

"I will. Bye."

Monique threw the phone on the bed, laid back on the pillow with her arm over her face. These people need to get their shit together. I'm tired of all of them, she thought.

Redemptive

"Who needs to get their shit together?" Amar asked, sounding like a parrot repeating her words.

"This whole family. Every time I turn around something else is going on. Another fire needs to be put out, another argument needs to be settled. I need a vacation."

"Take one. What's stopping you? There has been a lot going on. Take a break. I got work. Call Sam and find somewhere for you two to go."

Monique jumped up. This was the best news she'd heard in a long time. Yep, that's exactly what she needed. She picked up the phone, called Sam, they both looked at possible dates and before the night was over, the two was booked on a cruise for the following weekend. Amar would be gone so it was perfect, and the family would just have to figure it all out.

####

When the weekend arrived, the kids came out to the house, along with Graham, who came back in town early just for the dinner. Amar had picked up some black angus ribeye steaks which had been marinating for the last two days. Monique couldn't understand why he spoiled the kids the way he did, but she didn't complain. It could very well be the other way around.

Shane, Ty, along with Camille and her kids filled the back patio. Graham helped Amar with the food and Monique sat watching the movements of each person looking for any signs of tension. She couldn't find any. Amar and Graham was grilling and drinking beer, Camille did spend more time with her brother than with Ty, but that wasn't out of the ordinary, while Ty floated around like she always did.

Monique decided to let the evening progress along naturally only stepping in if there was a need. Everybody did their own thing until dinner was ready. Monique even went to speak to a neighbor she hadn't seen in a while. Both husband and wife travelled for business and were rarely home, so they hadn't heard about Monique's attack until recently. She assured them she was fine and Amar had reported it to the neighborhood watch for added patrol. They promised to get together the next time they were in town and all went on their way. When Monique returned, dinner was ready and they sat down to eat. The men found a game, so the TV replaced the music that was playing earlier. The sun was starting to set which made the solar lights illuminate their surroundings.

Watching each individual person starting with Shane who set to her left who was clueless about his wife, then there was Ty who was her normal chatty busy self, Graham, who kept watching Camille, Amar, the grandkids, then Camille, who was to her right. They made small talk about life in general, their lives, updates on the grandkids, and then Ty made her big announcement; she got a raise at work. Monique thought Camille would choke when she heard the words.

"You alright, sis?" asked Shane.

"Yeah, I'm good, excuse me," she said rising from her seat to go in the house.

"What's up with her?" asked Shane sounding irritated now.

"Why don't you go see," Monique suggested.

"No, I'll go," Ty said, springing up like a jack in the box. "It's probably a girl thing."

"Well then you go," Shane said, I want nothing to do with that."

Ty didn't hesitate to go in the house to check on her sister in law. Graham looked at Monique. She quickly started talking about her upcoming cruise with Sam and how excited she was to get away. Shane was none the wiser and they continued to make small talk until Monique decided she should go in the house and check on Camille and Ty. As soon as she entered the house,

Monique heard the shattering of glass. Picking up the pace to find the noise, she heard the women arguing in the living room.

"What the hell?" Monique yelled as she entered the living room but stopped to see the two women fighting and a vase broken. "Hey, hey…..break this shit up now!"

It wasn't long before the men came in to see what was going on. Shane grabbed Ty and Graham wrapped Camille in a bear hug.

"Somebody needs to tell me what the hell is going on and why you feel the need to tear up my house! Monique yelled.

"Let's go home Shane, your sister is crazy," yelled Ty. I won't stay here another minute," she said panting after each word.

"Good, take your thieving ass on outta here," Camille yelled back.

"Wait, what? What are you talking about Camille?" asked Shane while trying to restrain his wife.

"Ask your wife. Let her raggedy ass tell you. Let me go daddy, I'm getting my kids and I'm going home."

Redemptive

"No Camille, you are not driving home like this. Come let's go outside."

"Don't take her outside Graham, the kids are out there, take her upstairs, Monique said." Graham escorted Camille upstairs until Monique could calm the situation down. Stepping over broken glass and a coffee table that had been knocked over during the scuffle the two were soon out of site.

"You got this Mon? I'll go check on the kids," Amar asked which startled Monique who'd forgotten he came in with them.

"Yeah, go head. I got this."

Breathing deep to catch her breath, Monique looked at Shane and then Ty. Pissed beyond measure at the fact that this mess was brought to her house, now she was forced to deal with something that had nothing to do with her. Not to mention that shit in her house was now broken, like she lived in the hood.

"Sit down!" Monique ordered after she was alone with Shane and Ty. Without saying a word, the two sat in complete obedience. Monique's nerves were too raw for her to take a seat. Walking back and forth biting on her nails trying to find the words to start this crazy ass conversation she finally started.

"Ty, I am going to give you the chance to tell your husband what just happened between you and Camille. I'm not going to allow you to go another day playing this game you've been playing for some time now. It has gone on long enough, but it stops tonight."

"What are you talking about Ma…..just tell me," Shane asked sounding aggravated.

"Actually Shane, Camille should be telling you, but I don't think it's a good idea for her to come back down here right now."

"Without saying a word, Shane ran up the stairs."

"Damn, this ain't gone be good," said Monique.

"You just couldn't stay out of it, could you Monique? Didn't nobody ask you to open your mouth and say nothing!"

"Who the hell you raising your voice at Ty! This shit wouldn't have happened if you didn't spend your life taking things that didn't belong to you, in order to live like the Joneses. Besides, that's my son. How long did you think we were gonna sit back and let you destroy everything he is working so hard to build. Girl bye."

"I'm not going away that easy, Monique. That ain't gone happen. Me and Shane will work this out. Watch, you just watch."

Redemptive

The footsteps coming down the stairs got both their attention. When Shane came down the last step, without hesitation he grabbed Ty by the arm. "Let's go," was all he said. The two stormed passed Monique like a bolt of lightning and before Monique could say anything, they were gone. A few seconds later, she could hear the screeching of tires leaving her driveway. Graham came down the stairs a few minutes later.

"Well at least he knows," he said as he joined Monique in the disheveled living room. He's mad as hell and you can't blame him, but he asked Camille to show him the paperwork."

"What's that about?" Monique looked at Graham half puzzled.

"You know your son, he probably wants to leave no doubt in his mind going forward. One thing I do know is it's going to be some hell in that house tonight."

"That girl is clueless, Graham. Her ass was down hear blaming me for being involved."

"What?"

"Yeah. Enough of that, how's Camille?"

"You probably should check on her, she's really upset and I think it would be good for her and the kids to stay here tonight.

"I ag…..Before Monique could finish the sentence, Amar and the kids came pouncing through the door.

"We good in here?" Amar asked pausing before letting the kids loose. "It's getting a little chilly out so I decided to bring them in."

Monique got up to meet them in the kitchen, while Graham cleaned up the mess left behind. "Who wants hot chocolate?" Monique asked trying to distract them from the scene behind her.

Later when the children were settled, Monique went upstairs to check on Camille. Lying across the bed, eyes swollen from the tears and her body in the fetal position, Camille hugged a pillow as Monique came and sat on the bed.

"How you feeling?" Monique asked watching her daughter trying to gather her words.

"This is some messed up stuff, Ma. I hate what this is doing to Shane, but I'm tired of Ty acting like she can keep doing this kind of stuff and get away with it."

Redemptive

"I know. Your dad is going over there to make sure everything is okay. Shane was pissed when he left. I don't want anything to pop off with this craziness."

"Me either. Should I have told him the rest? I wasn't sure how far to go."

"Hell no! This was enough for one night."

Chapter 16

The Decision

Several days had gone by since the incident at Monique's house and she still hadn't heard from Shane or Tychia. Graham called later that night after he checked on them and told her they seemed okay. Monique tried contacting them both, but the phones went to voice mail. Telling herself they would have to work it out she turned her attention to her own situation. She'd been thinking on how to confront the pastor while being convinced there had to be more than her and Cyrus as his victims. How could she find out? What did she need to do to bring this to the forefront? She wasn't sure, but the cruise was in a couple of days and Sam would have to talk it out with her over several shots.

Monique pulled the suitcases from the closet for her and Amar. It was his weekend to be with Paulina so

Redemptive

they could pack together. While in the closet getting the suitcases, she could hear Amar on the phone, his voice sounding agitated. "What do you mean?" she heard him ask. "When did this happen? Why in the hell nobody called me until now?"

Stepping out of the closet, Monique stood with a look of concern on her face. Whatever it was didn't sound too good. Sliding the suitcases to one side of the closet with her foot, she waited for Amar to get off the phone. Sitting on the side of the bed after hanging up the phone, Monique waited for him to speak. When a few minutes went by and he still hadn't said anything, she walked around to his side of the bed.

"Hey, what's going on?" Obviously concerned by the look on his face.

"Paulina had a stroke earlier today," he said almost under his breath, his head bowed.

"What? Why are they just now telling you?" Monique was almost yelling and immediately realized that wasn't helping the situation. She took a seat beside him on the bed, putting one arm on his shoulder. "What's the situation now," she asked in a much calmer voice.

"Stable for now. They say she is very weak."

"Are you leaving tonight. I can pack a bag for you."

Turning to look at Monique with a puzzled look on his face Amar tilted his head. "Since when did you start packing for me? And no, I am not going there tonight."

He was right Monique thought, she'd never packed a bag for Mr. Independent, she could barely pack for herself, but considering the situation, she thought she'd offer.

"Why aren't you going tonight?"

"I've worked all day and I don't feel up to the drive. Besides she's sedated and won't know I'm there anyway. I will leave in the morning."

"Should I cancel my trip?"

Turning to look at her again with the same puzzled look he had before, he asked, "Why would you do that?"

"To be here in case something happens."

"No, go on your trip and have a good time. Everything will be alright."

Now Monique looked at him confused. She didn't say anything but wondered what kind of messed up shit was this. They both sat quietly for a while when Amar finally told her to go pack, he would be fine. It took time for her to register what he'd said. When it did she

Redemptive

got up, picked up her suitcase from the closet and put it on the trunk at the foot of the bed. Amar was stretched out on the bed now with his arms behind his head looking up at the ceiling. She wasn't sure if he was praying or thinking, but decided he was thinking because he prayed on his knees.

The next morning when the alarm went off at 5:00 so Amar could say his morning prayers, Monique realized he was already up. The door to the bathroom was closed and the shower was running. She couldn't help but wonder if he'd slept much at all. Sitting up in the bed, pulling her knees to her chest, she saw his bag already packed and knew he hadn't slept. If he had, it wasn't for long. Within minutes she heard the shower shut off and Amar emerged from the bathroom, towel around his waist, the moisture glistening from his body where he hadn't dried off completely. She wanted to hold him, to let him know she was there for him, but knew where it would lead, and it would cause him to miss his morning prayer. He had to be clean when he prayed, so Monique dismissed her intimate thought. Amar went into his morning ritual and she got up to get herself ready for work.

By the time she'd showered and dressed, he was ready to leave.

"Your coffee is already in your thermos. I am going to stop by the office before I head out. I will call you later." Amar kissed Monique on the forehead, patted her butt, while throwing his overnight bag over his shoulder.

"Wait a minute, why do you only have an overnight bag?"

"That's all I need, I will be back tonight or tomorrow," he said matter of factly.

"Why you not staying the weekend? It's your weekend to be there."

"I will call you and let you know." After that he was out the door and Monique could hear the start of his car. Shaking her head at the conversation that just took place, she sat at the bar sipping her coffee trying to assess the situation. The more she thought about it the more she couldn't make it make sense. After making her bed, starting a load of laundry and washing the morning dishes, she headed to the office. On her drive in, she thought about the nasty pastor and how to proceed with that situation. She would have to talk to her therapist about it at her next session. She'd helped her so much thus far, maybe it was time for them to discuss this. She had already said they would talk about a plan to pursue it, but it hadn't been brought up

Redemptive

again so far. Monique was running out of patience and needed some direction.

Despite the fact nobody in her family wanted her to pursue it, she had to do what was best for her and her healing. Who else was out there suffering in silence from the hands of this nasty man? It wasn't just for her, she kept telling herself, but for the many others that could be freed by her truth. Yep, that's what she was going to do. She just needed the plan.

Chapter 17

Next Steps

Monique and Sam's cruise was what she needed to help her gain perspective on many things. Through their many conversations between Tequila shots, they'd conquered the world's issues and through many tears, cut off and up several people in both their lives. They had been messy at times but enjoyed the trip and each other nonetheless. It wasn't all blubbery, they ate too much, danced too much and flirted way too much. Overall, it was a good trip and Monique was glad she'd gone. She did think in between her having a good time, about Amar and the situation with Paulina, but hadn't heard from him. Trying to contact him several times before leaving, Monique left it alone and chalked it up as no news is good news.

Redemptive

As close as Monique had been to Sam, she'd never told her about the molestation when it happened, and she wasn't exactly sure when she blocked it. When she finally did tell her and after they both cried about it, they were both ready to fight every man that passed them on the ship. But they started drinking and decided against it. They would make the best of the trip instead. Monique was grateful for the friendship and always knew Sam had her back no matter what.

When she returned home, Amar was there and was in much better spirits than when he left. He met Monique at the car when she'd pulled in the garage. Grabbing her, he kissed her passionately as if he truly missed her. Then he grabbed her bags and they headed in the house. He had thrown her completely off her game. She was going to play the "why haven't I heard from you card…..you said you were going to call me…..you said you were going to be home……..you said……" All the things she'd rehearsed in her mind, left and she couldn't think straight after such a welcome.

Entering the house candles were lit, the lights were dimmed, and music was playing. "What the hell did I just step in to?" she asked herself. Amar had disappeared into the bedroom and Monique could hear the shower running. All she wanted was a hot shower and the comfort of her bed. She would get both but not the way she thought.

After the welcome home greeting was over the two lay in bed, breathless, while Monique was still trying to figure out what just happened. Reminding herself to be in the moment to see where this was going, Amar began to talk.

"Paulina is doing better, but has a long road ahead," he said. "I'm not happy with the doctors there, but she wants to stay. I think they should be doing so much more for her."

Monique lay in silence, waiting to hear the rest of what he had to say. As much as she liked to talk, she knew it wasn't the time to spoil this moment.

"I missed you Mon, I'm glad you're home. This has been one hell of a week. It seems like lately our lives have been topsy turvy."

Glad to be lying in his arms so he couldn't see her face, Monique was shocked to hear those words. Amar usually didn't share his feelings like that. This situation with Paulina must have made him think about some things while she was away.

"Yeah, things have been a bit crazy lately. The trip was good, but I'm glad to be home. I missed you too."

Redemptive

"Are you ready for dinner?" Amar jumped up and headed toward the bathroom before Monique could answer. She was his kryptonite. He was rejuvenated and just like that their moment was over.

"Well damn, she thought, what just happened again?

######

On Monique's next visit with Dr. Meyers' she wanted to discuss the situation regarding the nasty pastor. She had also discussed it with Amar, and he reassured her he would support her in whatever decision she made. Feeling more confident now about moving forward, Monique wanted to hear what her therapist had to say.

"What do you hope to gain by exposing him now after all these years? Dr. Meyers asked Monique when she shared her news.

"I want him to be accountable for what he's done, not just to me but for the others who have not come forward yet."

"Are you ready for the backlash that could possibly come from all of this?"

"Are you trying to talk me out of it?" Monique was starting to become angry by Dr. Meyers line of questioning.

"Certainly not, but what I want you to understand, this is a powerful man we are talking about here and he won't go down without a fight. Are you prepared for the ridicule and humiliation he will try to bring to discredit you? It will be nothing compared to the questions I am asking you now. That's what I want you to understand and be prepared for. You will certainly need help emotionally through it."

"I know now most of my struggles in life have been because of what that man did to me. It is also why I now understand my not wanting anything to do with the church. Now that I am trying to get my life right with the Lord, I have to do this to get my peace. You've helped me see that, and I deserve it."

"You've come so far, but there is still a lot more we need to work on, I just don't want to see you have a set back from the progress we've made."

"I'm ready, Dr. Meyers, I promise you I am."

Chapter 18

Shane

Monique was feeling right pleased with her appointment with Dr. Meyers and decided she would stop and have a Mani Pedi to further enjoy her bliss. She hadn't felt this free in years and this new lease on life was making her feel empowered. It was almost as if she was seeing the world through a different set of eyes and she was becoming more open to possibilities. What she didn't miss though was the drama of the family. Her phone had been quiet for a couple of days and she was loving it. After her self-indulgence Monique headed home. She'd already told Amar she wouldn't be back in the office and would see him at home. Checking the clock on the dashboard, she still had a couple of hours before he would be home.

Singing along with a song on the radio, Monique was feeling pretty good. Pulling into the garage and entering the house, she decided to open some windows to let in fresh air. Next she turned on music and looked in the fridge to see what they would have for dinner. Amar in his normal let's be prepared fashion, had cut vegetables that were seasoned in a dish and chicken marinating in a sauce. "I will just put this on the grill when I think Amar is about home," she said to herself. Walking to the bedroom to change clothes, her cellphone rang. Looking at it, she saw it was Shane.

"Hey son."

"Hey. Where you at?"

"Home."

"I'm headed that way. I want to talk to you."

"Oka-a-a-y," Monique said slowly, unsure of what was about to interrupt her zen mode.

Before she knew it Shane hung up. It made her wonder. She hadn't heard from him since he snatched Ty by the arm and left that night. He hadn't answered any of her calls or anyone else's for that matter and now he wants to come and talk. Thinking while changing her clothes Monique played several

Redemptive

scenarios in her mind. "Girl get yourself together, you will know soon enough," saying to herself.

Sure enough, before Monique turned around good, the doorbell rang and Shane was at the door. "Were you out here already?" she asked as he came into the house.

"Yeah, I've been riding around for a while."

Looking at her son's face, she could see the tiredness in his eyes. Her first instinct was to hug him, but he wouldn't have liked that, so she resisted the urge.

"Sit down and tell me what's going on with you. I've tried to call you several times."

"I know. I just needed time to process what happened out here. I'm a be honest with you Ma, I'm struggling with it all. Right when I think me and that girl are on the same page, something else pops off with her."

"Nobody is perfect Shane. We all got issues."

"Really Ma, that's where you going with this?"

"I'm just saying. I know you are frustrated and hurt, but you all can work through this."

"I don't think I want to." Shane sat looking like the little boy who wanted to tie his own shoes without anybody showing him. He was determined to do it his way. Monique learned early on when he made up his mind to do something it was hard to change it.

"Don't be so quick to throw in the towel. Have you thought about counseling?" It's helping me with my issues. Maybe you should think……."

"Nope. I can't take another lie, I can't bail her out of another situation, and to do this to my sister, I can't forgive that. I don't think she wants help. I think she gets off doing this type of stuff."

"Why would you say that?"

"Because she keeps doing it!" Who in their right mind would jeopardize everything they have if they could stop it?"

Sensing her son's pain and hearing his anger, she decided to back off that approach. "Have you talked to her about how you're feeling? I don't mean you going off, but trying to understand what's going on with her, really?"

Shane looked at his mother with a look that showed her he wasn't interested in knowing the answer to that question. He was done and it showed all over him.

"What are you going to do?"

Redemptive

"I'm not exactly sure yet, I just wanted you to know what I was thinking."

"I hate hearing it, but I will respect your decision. Where you heading now?"

"Going to see Camille. I don't want her to think I'm mad at her, cause I'm not. I'm just mad at the situation."

"That'll be good. It will make her feel better, I'm sure."

Monique walked Shane to the door and hugged him this time as he left. Standing in the doorway watching him get in his car and drive off, her heart ached. This wasn't what she wanted for him, but she also knew it would come out sooner or later. She was glad that was all he knew, at least for now.

Chapter 19

Pastor Daniels

Pastor Daniels had made a name for himself in the church arena. Nationally known, bestselling author, dynamic speaker, community outreach leader, sat on several boards, recipient of numerous awards, featured in several magazines, was a faithful husband and beloved father. A pillar in the community. Everyone loved him, well almost everyone.

Every winter his church would take in the homeless, feed and clothe them. Every Spring and Summer there were hundreds of kids who benefited from his church's benevolence to attend youth camp. It had been a tradition from which he carried on from his days of being a youth pastor leading several hundred souls to Christ. He was proud of that feat and bragged of it often.

Redemptive

He had discipled several young ministers over the years and he was considered a spiritual father to many. There wasn't much you couldn't say about Pastor Daniels without someone co-signing on his accomplishments. His ministry was broadcast over several TV and Radio stations and the more Monique heard about him the more she felt sick to her stomach. Late one night while flipping through the channels she saw an advertisement for a big revival he was having at his church. He was inviting all to come and they were looking for volunteers to help. It was going to be a huge event. There she sat watching this monster standing there in a robe and all his bling, smiling at the camera like he was Jesus about to walk on water.

"Your time is coming Mister, just you wait and see. I promise this will be your last revival. You will be the one needing to be revived," she said speaking to the image on the screen.

That night Pastor Daniels invaded Monique's dreams, bidding her to come. Tossing and turning in her sleep, she kept seeing him with his hand outstretched toward her, telling her to come to him. He was the only one who could save her. Waking up in a cold sweat and feeling sick to her stomach, Monique ran to the bathroom and after a few minutes of hovering over the toilet, green slime came spewing from her mouth.

Waves after waves of the green slime kept erupting from her mouth like a volcano. When it was finally over, Monique slumped to the floor, completely limp and exhausted. She'd never encountered anything like that in her life, even on one of her drinking binges, she'd never had that happen. She was confused but relieved all at the same time, and for the first time since she could remember, felt totally and completely free. It would be hard to describe the feeling to anyone because it would be hard to explain. All she knew was she felt like a new person and a new life was waiting for her.

#####

Monique hadn't talked to Cyrus in several weeks, which was unusual for them, but she'd been busy with her life and apparently he had too. One day on her way home from work, she called him for a change. He immediately picked up.

"Girl, I was just thinking about you," he didn't waste any time saying when he answered the phone.

"Hey Cyrus, what's going on?"

"Moni, I been thinking about our last conversation a lot, and I want you to know I heard you, but I think I'm going to leave for a while. Get a new start. I know you ain't gone like it, but I gotta do this for me."

Redemptive

Rolling her eyes in her head, Monique took a deep breath. This wasn't the conversation she wanted to have today. Maybe it was best he left for a while. It would eliminate the weight she always carried when she talked to him.

"That's your life Cyrus, do what you want to do with it. All I'm saying to you is running ain't gone solve your issues. It's where you're standing that determines how you see things.

"I knew you were going to be mad."

"Why would I be mad about your life? You have to do what's best for you. Right now I'm not sure you know what it is."

"You talk to Aunt Geneva?"

"No, I haven't really talked to anybody, why? What is she up to now?"

"She's all excited, she's going to volunteer over at Pastor Daniels' church for the revival they having next month."

"What did you say Cyrus?"

"She's going to volunteer for the revival everybody's talking about."

"The nerve of that woman!" Monique was furious. The peace and calm she'd experienced flew right out of the window. "This is why I can't get my life right with the Lord!"

"What Moni?"

"Why the hell would she do anything at that church after what that man did to me?"

"Girl, you know I try to block that shit out of my mind. But she's wrong for that. That's messed up Moni."

"You need to stop blocking it and go get some help before you lose your mind Cyrus. Once you lose it you can't get it back, and that son of a biscuit bread eater ain't worth that!"

"I ain't strong like you Moni, I can't just talk about it like it's nothing. It's a very big deal to me, besides I don't want people to look at me differently.

"Different from what Cyrus?" When Monique ask the question, she realized she may have crossed the line with her cousin. She didn't say it to make him feel bad, she wanted him to know people already look at him a different way. "All I'm saying is we all have issues, we can choose to get help or continue to live the way we are and stay the same. I'm choosing to get help. I want

Redemptive

a better life and I am gonna do what it takes to get it. I owe this to myself."

"What are you saying?"

"I'll tell you later. Let me run, I'm home and I need to make a phone call."

When Monique got in the house and got herself together, she called Geneva.

"Hello."

"Geneva, are you home?"

"Yeah, I'm home," Geneva said hesitantly after hearing the tone in Monique's voice.

"I'm coming by. You and I need to talk."

"Okay. See you when you get here."

Monique slammed the phone down on its base and flopped on the bed fuming. At all cost she had avoided this conversation but now it was past time to have it. Her not wanting to go there with her mama, but her mama walking around like she deserves the "Mother of the Year award," was too much for Monique to sit quietly by and remain silent. Normally she would shower and change into house clothes, but not today. Strapping on her backpack and grabbing her keys from the bowl by the door, she headed to Geneva's. If this went according to her plan she would still beat Amar home from work.

When Monique arrived at Geneva's, she was standing in the door waiting for her. Monique sat in the car and stared at the woman who was suppose to be there for her, not go support the enemy; the man who stole her innocence, her self-esteem, destroyed her ability to trust, and anything else she could think of. Turning off the ignition and stepping out of the car, she took a very deep breath as she walked toward the front door. It was a struggle trying not to let her body language show how mad she was. The closer she got to the house the harder it was to hide it. Her stride was calculated but intentional and before long, met Geneva at the door.

"Hey," she said walking past her mama.

"Hey," Geneva said in a guarded response.

"You want something to drink?"

"No. I'm good."

"Go head, sit down," Geneva motioned for Monique to take a seat. Monique sat in the chair across from Geneva and didn't hesitate to start the conversation.

"I understand you are going to volunteer at Daniels church." Monique didn't intend for her words to be so

Redemptive

blunt, but they were out now and she couldn't take them back.

"Yeah, I thought it would be a good way to volunteer some time."

Shaking her head in an attempt to unhear what she just heard, Monique tried not to hold her breath. "Why in the hell would you go and do anything at that man's church, Geneva?" Not waiting for her to answer Monique continued, "See this is what I'm talking about with you. You know what that man did to me and I know you know because Cyrus told me he told you, and you would do something like this! What is wrong with you?" The anger was rising from Monique like the incident had just happened.

Geneva sat across from her daughter, eyes wide and her mouth trying to find the right words to say. Before she was able to speak, Monique started in again.

"This is why I can't have a relationship with you! You don't get why I feel the way I do about this. You and the rest of the family telling me to get over this is never going to happen and for you to go over there like everything is alright pisses me off and is a slap in my face. What mother does that to her child?" Monique's words sounded like she was rambling and running together with the speed of lightning, but felt the point was being made.

"Don't question my motherhood Monique, because I was a good mother to you. You never wanted for anything. I made sure you had everything you needed."

"What I needed was a mother to protect me from people like Daniels, that's what I needed. You were so quick to send me off somewhere, but look at how that turned out. So now that you know, you still haven't addressed the fact that it happened. For the life of me I can't make this shit make sense with you."

"Do you want me to talk to him, Monique?"

"Hell no! Why would you go and talk to him? What's that gon do? Naw, I got this Geneva. I can fight my own battles. What I want you to do is understand why this is important to me. How it would be helpful if you knew what supporting ME looked like instead of living in denial and thinking you were the perfect mother. That didn't happen Geneva for the record. I want you to get that. I'm not trying to make you feel bad, but this charade has lasted long enough. You've known about this now for a while and you still have yet to ask me who I am in all of this. Why is it so hard for you to be concerned about me?"

Redemptive

"I just want things to be okay between us Monique. That's all. I won't go to the revival, if that's what you want."

Monique could see Geneva trying to fight back tears, but they were starting to fall down her cheeks. Refusing to be moved by what she saw, unsure if they were for her or that she might miss the revival.

"I talked to mama about this and she told me to leave it alone, so I didn't say anything."

"Really Geneva, you talked to grandma, but you couldn't talk to me? You keep proving my point over and over again. You don't know how to be there for me, you just never have."

"What do you want me to do, Monique. Tell me and I will do it."

"Nope, you gotta figure this out on your own."

Chapter 20

The Confrontation

The sound of wind beating against the house woke Monique from a deep sleep. It took blinking her eyes several times to see her surroundings and realize where the noise was coming from. Still half groggy from her peaceful sleep, she rolled over to see Amar still in bed. What time is it? she asked herself trying to focus her eyes once again to see the clock on the dresser across the room. It was odd for Amar to still be in bed. He was an early riser with his morning prayers and also Monique couldn't help but wonder if something was wrong. Moving closer to make sure he was breathing, she felt relief when he moaned at her touch. Closing her eyes, Monique was relieved to know at least physically he was fine. Still, it was past the time for his morning prayer and the concern lingered in her mind. She wouldn't worry too

Redemptive

much, it was a Saturday morning and they didn't have anything pressing to do but be ready for the house cleaners to arrive at 11:00. There were six hours yet before they came.

Monique lay now on her back staring at the ceiling while listening to the wind blow. It sounded angry like the anger she felt regarding several things in her life right now. So many things had happened to her over the course of her life, some things she may have put herself in the position for them to happen but others, not so much. Why Geneva couldn't understand how the role of a mother is vital to a child growing up and the responsibility a mother carries was beyond her. She thought about Cyrus and how messed up his life was and wished he could get it together, but you can't want more for someone than they want for themselves. Then it was the issue of Shane and Ty. She wished the family never had to be put in the situation of having to cover for Ty and jeopardize her relationship with her son. "*My Lord,*" Monique thought, why are all these things running through my mind so early in the morning?" Then her mind went to the upcoming revival and Pastor Daniels. Immediately she knew what to do with her day. Rising from her position to sit on the side of the bed, Monique turned to look at Amar, he'd barely moved. "What is going on with him this morning? Is it

Paulina?" Walking into her closet, Monique grabbed a pair of yoga pants and a t-shirt and headed upstairs to walk on the treadmill. She turned on the TV and a severe storm warning was in effect according to the weather report. Flipping through the channels she found a movie that looked interesting and began her walk. After a few minutes she had to adjust the volume because of the howling wind. Before long, her hour was up and she headed to the shower hoping by the time she finished Amar would be up stirring around.

When she made her way downstairs after the shower, Amar was in the kitchen cooking.

"Good morning, she said when she saw him. I was wondering if you would be up by the time I finished my workout."

"I didn't sleep well last night so I thought I'd sleep in this morning."

"I was thinking this morning that today is the day to go over to see Daniels."

Amar raised his eyes slowly to Monique while he flipped pancakes. "Are you sure you're ready? What does your therapist say about you making this move now?"

Redemptive

"There's never going to be a good time or right time, Amar. I just have to do it."

"Do you want me to come with you?"

"I think so, but I don't want you to come in. Just be there for me when it's over."

Amar didn't say anything but looked at Monique confused. As if reading his mind, she continued her conversation. This has to be between me and Daniels and not you adding to it. Do you understand?"

"Yes. I told you I would do whatever you wanted me to do. So, I will stay in the car until it's over."

"Thanks. Can we leave right after breakfast? I want to get to the church before he leaves. He won't be there long today since it's Saturday."

"Sure." When Amar finished cooking breakfast they sat at the bar and enjoyed their time together. Monique rinsed the dishes for the dishwasher and got dressed for her visit. She and Amar drove into the city to confront the nasty pastor. It didn't even bother her that the wind was fierce, the storm she was about to walk into was going to be greater she felt.

Amar held Monique's hand as he drove, and he could feel her tension. The silence was another indicator of her tenseness because Monique was never short on words. The skyline of the city was coming into view, faster than she wanted it to, but this was something that had to be done. Her hope was the weight of her past would be lifted after her confrontation with Daniels. With each turn Monique tighten her grip in Amar's hand. When they finally arrived in front of the church that took up an entire block, she let go of his hand.

"Are you sure this is what you want?" asked Amar.

"I don't have a choice."

"You always have a choice, Mon."

"Not with this." Monique pulled the handle to open the door and stepped out of the truck. Looking back at Amar one last time, he whispered the words, "I love you," so in that moment she felt the strength to walk up the stairs and into Redemptive Life Baptist Church and face her abuser. It was what she'd expected, overwhelmingly large and empty with the exception of a handful of people decorating the stage and hanging banners in preparation of their revival. A middle-aged woman approached Monique and asked if she needed help.

"Yes, I'm here to see Pastor Daniels."

Redemptive

"Do you have an appointment?" asked the woman looking Monique up and down.

"No, ma'am, but I have some unfinished business to discuss with him."

The woman looked at Monique with a suspicious look on her face. "Pastor Daniels only sees people by appointment. Can someone else help you?"

"No ma'am," Monique repeated herself, this time her voice was stern, "it has to be Pastor Daniels.

"What's your name?"

"Monique Harper." Harper was the name she knew he'd recognize and not her married name.

"Okay, Ms. Harper, wait right here and let me see if he's available. Have a seat if you like."

Monique took a seat and watched the people continue in their various tasks while she waited on the woman to return. She thought about how such a slick and cunning man had been able to amass such a church in the name of the Lord. She couldn't dispute the fact the people loved him, thousands if not millions of people followed him, but she couldn't let this go.

When the woman returned to the sanctuary, there was another woman with her. Monique recognized her immediately as the pastor's wife. She had not anticipated this move.

"Hello, Ms. Harper," Mrs. Daniels said as she offered to shake her hand. "I understand you are here to see my husband."

"Yes, I am. It's regarding some old business." Monique was surprised by the cordial tone Mrs. Daniels displayed.

"Sure, I will take you to him, if you will just follow me." Monique looked at the woman who brought out the wife. "Thank you, ma'am," she said as she walked past her.

Monique followed the woman down a long hallway and around a corner to another one. The church was immaculately kept, she noticed as the walk seemed to be never ending, until they finally arrived at an office and went in.

"Have a seat, Ms. Harper, Mrs. Daniels said, motioning to a chair in front of a very large but feminine styled desk.

Monique's fight or flight senses kicked in at this point, but hesitantly she sat. Immediately the demeanor of the woman changed, and it caught Monique off guard.

Redemptive

"Now tell me Ms. Harper, what do you want with my husband?" This time the pleasantness from her voice disappeared.

"This is a matter regarding something that happened many years ago," Monique said trying to remain calm and not be intimidated by this woman.

"Listen lady, I don't have a lot of time here. What do you want? Money? Or do you have a long-lost child you want him to know about? Or better yet, you were one of his victims from back in the day? Which is it?"

All Monique could do was sit there dumbfounded. The beautiful woman who appeared before her just a few minutes ago, polished and refined, now looked tired and her eyes held a sadness about them even though her mouth was spewing something different. Before Monique could answered she continued.

"You are not the first and probably won't be the last, so what is it that you want? I can tell you right now, there isn't any more money for you to extort."

"I'm not looking for any money! Do you think what your husband has done to me and countless others can be silenced by money?"

"It has for many. What makes you so different?"

"It's not about the money. It's about me being free of this dark cloud that has been hanging over my life for years now. So, you know your husband's past and you stay with him anyway? What does that say about you?"

"That's none of your business."

"You are correct. It's not. All I want is to face my abuser, to be able to get closure on this part of my life and move on from this."

"Who do you think you are fooling? I've fallen for that trick too many times before. It's not gonna happen this time."

"I'm not fidna argue with you and I don't mean you no disrespect. But I was trying to do this the easy way which isn't working. I am prepared to bring this to the public and go to the police if I have to. Then it will only open the door for the other victims who have remained silent all these years to come forward. I feel sorry for you that his sickness has become your problem and your children's problem, but you know what's done in the dark will come to the light. I am not afraid to tell what happened to me."

"So you are threatening me!" shouted Mrs. Daniels.

"It's not a threat. I promise you it's not."

Redemptive

"Why are you doing this now, after all these years? Mrs. Daniels had moved from behind the desk to sit on the corner of the desk with her arms folded.

"I recently remembered the molestation. Apparently I blocked it for many years. Why do you continue to protect him? What if it was one of your children this happened to? Do you know it wasn't just with girls, it was with boys too?"

"Get out of here and don't you come back!"

Monique had never encountered an evil spirit, but the sound that came from Mrs. Daniels could have surely been one. Her voice sounded like it was almost a growl.

Turning to leave the office, Monique stopped when she reached the door. "I really feel sorry for you and your family, because this man has destroyed many lives. I wouldn't lie to you about that. And based on what you've shared, you know who he really is, and you have to decide when you have had enough. If you haven't and I know you've been married for many years now but get yourself tested."

"Don't come back here!" yelled Mrs. Daniels. Don't you ever come back here!

Monique tried to remember her way back to the sanctuary and it seemed longer than it did before. Finally, she reached the door to the sanctuary, picked up her stride and made her way outside. Stopping to breathe fresh air, Monique suddenly felt weak. Holding on to a rail for support, before she knew it Amar ran up the stairs to meet her.

"Hey, hey, are you alright?" he asked while putting his arm around her for support.

Nodding her head yes she leaned into him. Amar could feel her shaking underneath his grasp. Opening the door for her to get in the truck, he turned back to look at the church. There was a woman standing at the door who had been watching them. Walking around to get in the driver's side of the truck, he turned to Monique. "What happened in there?"

"The coward wouldn't come out, so I met with his wife."

"Did you ask to meet with her?"

"No. This old lady told me she was going to get him but the wife came out instead."

"Let's get out of this neighborhood," Amar said looking up at the doors to the church now seeing more people gathered watching them.

Chapter 21

The Visit

When Monique and Amar left the church, they went to one of their hole in the wall diners to talk. Monique gave him a blow by blow account of what happened, and Amar couldn't believe the cover up that had taken place and the wife knew it!

Monique only ordered water, she was too wound up to eat anything. The two sat and talked then finally made their way home. The drive home was different than when they left earlier that day. They were engaged in conversation about their next move.

"I told her I was prepared to go public with this."

"Are you?" Amar glanced over at Monique.

"Hell, I don't know Amar. I got caught up in the heat of the moment." They both laughed. "Don't get me wrong, I am not going to let it rest. But I do feel sorry for the lady though."

"Why? Mean as you say she was, why feel sorry for her?"

"Cause, I'm sure she didn't know what she was getting herself into when she married him. She is just probably trying to defend her future and what dignity she has left."

"That ain't your problem Mon, so don't make it yours.

The wind was still blowing when they arrived home, and the rain was starting to fall. Monique forgot all about the storm coming. They headed straight to the patio to stack and store the chairs, cushions, lanterns and candles in case the storm was as bad as they predicted.

They barely made it in the house when the doorbell rang. When Monique looked at the security screen, all she could say was, "What the hell?"

"What is it Mon?" asked Amar coming from one of the rooms down the hall.

"It's Daniels! What the hell is he doing here?"

Redemptive

"He bet not come with no shit!" Amar who was 6'4"and knew all about that street life was not a man to be easily intimidated. Monique wasn't worried about anything happening but wanted him to remain calm. "Let's see what he wants," said Amar walking toward the door.

"Calm down Amar," she said following behind him. "Why don't you let me get it."

The doorbell rang a second time before Monique could reach the door.

Looking out the side panel of the door, Monique could see he was standing at the door alone. His driver was still seated in his black Maybach parked in front of her house.

Opening the door, Monique was unusually calm at seeing Pastor Daniel up close and personal after all these years. She was really surprised that his entourage wasn't with him. But then again, she was sure he probably didn't want them in his business like that.

"Ms. Harper, I understand you came to see me earlier and I was unavailable. I apologize for that. May I come in please?"

Monique looked at the perfectly starched man who stood before her and for a split second, second guessed her position until she heard Amar's voice behind her inviting the man in. Surprised by Amar's presence, the pastor seemed hesitant now to enter. Monique stepped to the side to allow the pastor to enter their home.

"You have a very lovely home," Pastor Daniels said, suddenly appearing nervous.

"Thanks," Amar answered before Monique could gather her thoughts to respond.

"So you drove clear across town to come out here to see me, someone who does not attend your church, nor have I been in touch with you to know anything about me?" asked Monique after they all sat.

"That's what having a well-paid assistant can do for you, find a needle in a haystack," he said trying to bring light to the moment. But his attempt at any humor was failing.

"Is it possible, Ms. Harper to speak alone."

"No!" Amar shut that possibility completely down.

"My husband is fully aware of the molestation, so anything you have to say you can certainly say it in front of him."

It was more than obvious and uncomfortable for Daniels at this point that he wasn't prepared for this

Redemptive

situation, nor for Monique to be so bold with her accusation.

"Well…..well….Ms. Harper, my wife told me about your conversation and as you can imagine she is quite upset. Now those are some strong allegations you have made to her, and quite frankly I don't ever recall you or the things you mentioned to her. Can you please tell me when this allegedly happened?"

Oh, he's good, Monique thought, slick as oil, but he wasn't going to slide his way out of this.

"You don't remember, huh? Well, let me help you remember. Summer camp, the administration building, sending my cousin out so we could be alone"……Before she could finish, the revelation was apparent by his facial expression.

Let's see how he worms his way out of this, Monique thought.

"I was a very different man back then and made some terrible mistakes. I'm not that man anymore, Ms. Harper. Please forgive me for any wrong I've done to you."

The words struck like a lightning bolt and made her fall back in her chair. What was happening here? Never would she have imagined hearing those words ever from him. This was too easy. What was he up to? Was this an attempt to protect his legacy by offering an apology and hoping it all would go away. She didn't think so, surely he couldn't believe that. This move certainly threw her off and while trying to regain her composure to respond, Amar stepped in and became her mouthpiece.

"Hold up Rev, you came out here with this half-assed apology to my wife like you pushed her down on the playground or something and that's it? What about the things you stole from her like trust, and her ability to love like a woman is suppose to, or her relationship with God? Naw partner, it ain't going down like that."

Monique looked at Amar and was shocked by his response. The man of few words managed to come to her rescue when she was at a loss for them. When Monique turned to look at the pastor, the man who is always confident in the pulpit, now looked like a helpless, uncertain older man who was in need of help. She wondered what his church members would say if they saw him right now.

"I mean neither one of you any disrespect," Pastor Daniels spoke after Amar's words. I have hurt a lot of people, especially my wife, who didn't deserve any of this and when she told me about your visit, I knew it

Redemptive

was time to start righting some of the wrongs I've done."

"How can you preach the gospel in the Lord's house knowing what you've done to his people? And how many has it been, because I know for a fact it wasn't just me or just girls."

The pastor's eyes widen like saucers. Monique could tell by the shift in his body language he wasn't prepared for the knowledge she just shared. With a look of utter embarrassment, he dropped his head.

"Wow! This is so farfetched that I can't make this shit up, Monique said under her breath. *"What really is happening right now? The poor man looks like he needs comforting,"* but her thoughts were interrupted by his next response.

"I came here in good faith, trying to make things right with you Ms. Harper, but I will not sit here and be humiliated by the lies you speak!" Standing as if to leave, Amar stood too, to let him know this is not your church or your house and he wasn't going to manipulate them in any way.

"You don't get to decide when or if Monique forgives you for what you did to her. That's her decision, not yours, Rev. What you need to worry about is how many more people are going to come forward. I know you have had people come to you and your wife in private, for money or because they were embarrassed, but that is not the case here. We don't have a problem going public. Cause see, we don't care about your reputation. Ain't that right Monique?" Touching Monique on the shoulder to get her to respond, she knew Amar was now angry with the foolishness the pastor was throwing their way.

"Yes, Pastor Daniels. We are not looking for anything from you except for you to acknowledge your wrongdoing publicly. The people have a right to know what you've done along with the people you have victimized. If you are the pastor the world believes you are, then you know what you need to do. I know God forgives our sins, but it can't stop there. That doesn't give you the right to cover them up."

"Thank you for your time, Ms. Harper, and?....... turning to Amar realizing he didn't get his name. "I think it's best for me to go now."

Walking toward the door, Pastor Daniels turned to Monique one last time. "I heard what you said, Ms. Harper, but it's not that easy. I will have to seek the direction from the Lord."

"Me too," was all Monique could say in response to his statement.

Redemptive

Monique and Amar watched the man who was self-confident when he arrived, leave a totally different way. His demeanor was not the same now and all they could do was look at each other. When they closed the door, all she could say was, "What the hell just happened?"

"That's why I don't deal with the church. This is one time I am glad for my Muslim faith."

"Yeah right, Amar let's make this about you," Monique said as she walked to the kitchen to pour herself a glass of wine. "Thanks for having my back though, I appreciate it. I was so caught off guard with that man. I never expected that to happen."

"No worries, Mon. That's what I'm here for. I wasn't about to let him or anyone else disrespect you or me. You never have to worry about that."

"You want a glass of wine?"

"No, I'll grab a beer."

The two sat at the bar in the kitchen drinking and rehashing the conversation with the good Pastor Daniels. Monique knew the storm had been brewing outside was nothing compared to what she'd experienced that day or what was about to come.

######

When Pastor Daniels got in the car, he called his wife.

"How did it go?" she asked after hearing his voice.

"Not as I planned. This is a tough one, she's not going away, I don't think."

"Did you offer her money?"

"She doesn't want money, and based on where she lives, it doesn't look like she needs it. Besides her husband isn't one to be pushed around either."

"Damn! What are you gonna do?"

"I don't know just yet, but I will not let anybody destroy what I've built!

"Don't you mean we?" You didn't do this alone."

"You know what I mean. I'll see you shortly."

Frustrated with the inability to control this situation, Pastor Daniels punched the seat with his fist. He had to figure out how to handle Monique Harper. Revival was coming and he wouldn't let her or anyone else interfere with his ministry or the legacy he'd built.

Chapter 22

The Big News

Redemptive Life Baptist Church spent the better part of a year planning their upcoming revival. They'd lined up some of the biggest names in the gospel industry as well as well-known pastors. They'd spared no expense for the week. The various committees had taken care of everything from travel, accommodations, meals, entertainment, gifts and more.

Pastor and First Lady Daniels hadn't spoken much more about Monique Harper and poured all their energy into the revival. They made many ads for the event along with radio and TV interviews to boost attendance. The duo was a powerhouse. They'd spent years building the ministry, making many sacrifices along the way and it had paid off for them in spades. The ministry was flourishing beyond their wildest dreams and despite the money paid in extortions, they still were living large.

Their children had been educated. They'd traveled the world several times over, started various businesses, mentored hundreds of ministers and their spouses, earned honorary degrees, fed the homeless, given to countless organizations, charities, and built the ministry as a result. The sacrifice had been great, but the reward was much greater.

####

The night before the revival, the Daniels' had dinner and headed to bed early. The next day would be full and they wanted to be well rested. Neither wanted to talk about the elephant in the room, but Mrs. Daniels brought it up.

"Do you think she will try something at the revival?"

"I've increased the security so it will be difficult if she did."

"I just wish I knew what she was up to."

"Don't go borrowing trouble honey."

"I'm not. Should I pay her a visit?"

Redemptive

"No! Absolutely not! Leave that woman and her crazy husband alone. They could have a change of heart you know."

"Not based on what you told me, nor did I get that from my encounter with her. I just want it to be over, whatever it is."

"Well I'm afraid that is out of our hands."

"It doesn't have to be."

"What are you saying?"

Tilting her head to one side, with the light from the lamp lighting her face, Pastor Daniels could see the concern on his wife's face. The woman who he'd married thirty years ago had stood by his side through the controversies, the blackmail, and the like, was asking, looking to him for reassurance and he couldn't give it. He didn't know what Monique Harper was going to do. He had done everything he knew to do but pray. He hadn't prayed to the One who could bring him answers, because if the truth be told, he'd lost his faith a long time ago. Ministry had become a job to him now, not a passion, and he was tired. Tired of the responsibility and tired of living the lie.

"There are ways to make it all go away," his wife said.

"Have we become those people?" he asked sadly.

"Yes, we did. A long time ago, I'm afraid."

"I'm sorry."

"Me too."

Later that night after his wife was asleep, Pastor Daniels went downstairs to his study, wrote a letter to his wife, to his kids and to his church. After that, he opened the locked box he kept in his bottom drawer, pulled out the .22 caliber handgun, held it to his temple and pulled the trigger.

Hearing a noise, Mrs. Daniels jumped to an upright position. Feeling for her husband in the darkness, she realized he wasn't there. Turning on the light to find her bedroom shoes, she opened the door and listened. The house was deathly quiet. Making her way down the stairs slowly while still listening for any movement, she finally reached the bottom step. She could see the door to her husband's office cracked and a light drew her to where she found her husband's lifeless body. It was bent over the desk where he'd written countless sermons. The gun lay to the right of his hand. She stood motionless but mesmerized by the image that lay before her. Anticipating a cry, or a scream would come, but it didn't. Almost in a zombie like trance, Mrs. Daniels made her way over to the phone on the desk and dialed 9-1-1. The next call was

Redemptive

to her children and then the head of security from the church.

They all arrived within minutes of each other. The paramedics checked for a pulse and pronounced the pastor DOA. The children were crying, but Mrs. Daniels remained emotionless.

Baxter Findley, a retired cop and the head of security for Redemptive knew the police chief and made the call to him on the drive to the Daniels' estate. The chief arrived shortly after everyone else. After looking over the scene, he waited for the paramedics to remove the body. He stood in the hallway asking Baxter questions. The men talked in hush tones, assessing what they thought may have happened before talking to Mrs. Daniels.

#####

The news spread through the media and the church community like wildfire.

Chapter 23

The Aftermath

Amar woke Monique when he heard the news regarding Pastor Daniels. The story was on every channel as breaking news. Sitting up still half-asleep, Monique listened to the reporter as images of the pastor, the church, and his family scrolled in the background. Holding her hand over her mouth, it was hard to believe what she was hearing.

"It's not your fault Mon, so don't even go there," Amar tried to assure her. "That man had been troubled for some years. He had to have been."

Still sitting in the same position, she could hear Amar talking but couldn't comprehend his words. Tears began to fall from her face, stopping at the point where her hand still covered her mouth and forming small puddles.

Redemptive

Monique's phone rang but she maintained her position. Amar stood watching the news as if he was hearing it for the first time. Talking to the TV and Monique at the same time he hadn't realized her current state. It finally registered that Monique wasn't responding. Looking back at her he saw the tears.

"Mon, don't do this to yourself. Don't give that dude any more power than he's already had over you all these years." He held her in his arms, rocking her back and forth. "You didn't make him pull that trigger, he made that choice on his own."

The phone continued to ring. Monique lay in Amar's arms and cried like she'd never cried in her life. First of all, she wasn't a crier, so this was really new for her. Somehow she felt cheated, robbed once again to have a say in something that affected her life. On the other hand though, she got to face her abuser, hear him ask for forgiveness, but would that be enough? She didn't know, only time and sessions with Dr. Meyers would tell.

When Monique and Amar woke from their nap the story of the pastor was still playing. Monique tried to open her eyes which felt like she'd been cold cocked in both of them. How much crying did she really do for them to feel this way? Finding the strength to get out of bed to make it to the bathroom, she suddenly became aware that Amar wasn't there. That's odd, she thought, I didn't feel him get up. The house phone and her cell phone were missing from her nightstand which made her wonder how many times had the phone rang for him to take them out of the room.

She made her way to the bathroom and almost screamed when she looked at the red swollen eyes staring back at her. "Damn girl, you look a mess!" Turning the water on for the shower and after adjusting the temperature, she stepped in. As motionless as she was when she heard the news, Monique stood under the shower head and let the water fall freely over her tired body and broken spirit. She wasn't sure how long she'd been standing there but the knock on the door got her attention.

"Hey Mon, you been in there for a while, you alright?" asked Amar.

"Yeah." Trying to snap out of the trance she apparently was in, Monique began washing her body and got out of the shower. Next she looked for her eyedrops to soothe her irritated eyes, brushed her teeth and got dressed. She couldn't hide forever, at some point she would have to face the world and the mess going on in it.

Redemptive

Amar had breakfast waiting for her. Trying to get out of eating, Monique couldn't resist Amar's famous grits and eggs, so she made herself take a few bites.

"What happens now?" asked Amar.

"Hell if I know. I can't believe he thought death was better than facing the truth. To put his family through this, his church, the community. What a coward."

"They were already going through it Mon, you don't think the church knew about his past life. You know the wife knew. They chose to look the other way. That's on them, not you."

"I know, but it still makes me sad that all the other people didn't get their time to face him, people like Cyrus and who knows who else."

"Speaking of Cyrus, he's called at least twenty times. You might want to give him a call and Geneva."

Monique looked up from eating the last bite of food she felt she could eat, when Amar said Geneva."

"Yep, she called a couple of times too."

"For what? To make me feel guiltier that I already do? No thanks."

"Well at least call Cyrus."

Monica Hailey Sharpe

"I will, but I need a little time before I do, knowing him I'm going to need every ounce of strength I can muster with him, he's probably a sloppy mess."

"Probably."

Chapter 24

Monique

Dr. Meyers was able to see Monique on Monday midmorning. The last few days had taken a toll on her, not just for herself, but Cyrus too. He had not taken the news well at all and was a mess all weekend. She avoided talking to Geneva to maintain a small portion of her sanity until she could meet with Dr. Meyers.

Monique loved the calming effects Dr. Meyers office had on her. The blues and yellows on the walls and the decorations always made her feel better during her sessions. So many things took place since her last visit and Monique knew this one would be intense.

Once she and Dr. Meyers made it through the pleasantries, Monique jumped right into her latest dilemma. Blow by blow trying to remember the details of her conversation with her mama, then going to the church and having the wife of the pastor lambast her for being another extortionist, and last but certainly not least, the visit before the pastor's death. Taking a deep breath after spewing it all out, Monique fell back onto the pillows on the sofa which had been perfectly placed.

"Well we certainly have a lot to cover today Ms. Harper. Let's start with the conversation with your mother. Do you feel she heard you and the points you were trying to make with her?" Dr. Meyers was about the same age as Monique with glowing brown skin, who was always professional and well put together. Monique admired her professionalism and her six-inch heels.

"No. All she kept wanting to do was fix everything. I don't want her to fix it, I just wanted her to hear me and leave the martyr syndrome alone."

"How do you see the relationship going forward?"

"Nowhere."

"Why, and before you answer, take the emotions and the disappointments out of the equation."

Lifting her head from the back of the sofa to give Dr. Meyers a look of concern, Monique paused, considered

Redemptive

the instructions and thought of a reason outside of those two things.

"Is it fair to say we always know how to handle situations that come in our lives unexpectedly, perfect?"

"No, but as a mother, she should know how to be there for her child."

"Says who?" You? Because you were violated?"

"No, because when she was told, she chose not to address it."

"Is that unforgivable?"

"No, but I also don't feel the need to have a relationship with her after this when all she had to say was, I'm sorry that happened to you."

"It may not be the right time yet for that to happen. All I ask is that you be open to the possibility when it presents itself."

Checking her watch, Dr. Meyers asked Monique if she needed a break since they just worked through their first hour. Choosing to get a cup of water, Monique was glad for the break knowing the next hour was going to be emotionally brutal.

Dr. Meyers and Monique talked through the situation regarding Pastor Daniels which a lot of what she said aligned with Amar's words when he tried to comfort her. It was raw emotion for Monique and it would be a while before complete healing would take place in that area. Maybe if he had not paid her the visit, she wouldn't have felt as bad, but he did, and she couldn't shake it.

There was so much more she needed to talk to Dr. Meyers about like Shane and Tychia and that whole fiasco. She couldn't spend the afternoon in session though, life was waiting for her and she was sure Dr. Meyers had other patients also.

On her drive to the office Monique thought about a lot of the things Dr. Meyer's said to her. Forgiveness being the main component. It's not for the other person, it is for you, so you can go on with your life. "Who do you need to forgive Monique, and who do you need to ask for forgiveness from?"

She hadn't thought about that part, maybe she'd played the victim more than she thought, but that was never any stance she wanted to take. She was nobody's victim, or was she?

She really was trying to be a better person. She had started going back to church and was really trying to

Redemptive

develop a relationship with the Lord. It was hard some days, but she was trying. In her trying though, she felt she was always stumbling with somebody else's mess, like Cyrus, Geneva, Shane and Ty, sometimes Amar, but she also knew the devil was busy.

What she desperately needed was a distraction from all the pastor stuff, so work would be it for now. They were always busy there and she could get completely lost in that. Monique was so engrossed in her thoughts she forgot to get lunch and was now back at work. Maybe something is in the fridge, she thought as she grabbed her bags from the backseat and walked into the building.

Chapter 25

Monique

While the world was preparing to celebrate the life of Pastor Daniels, Monique decided to have her own celebration of life. Dr. Meyers gave her a lot to think about and was right in a lot of ways about having expectations of others. She was solely responsible for her happiness. It didn't matter to her if Geneva didn't know how to apologize, or Cyrus was struggling with his, or whether Shane and Tychia could work out their issues. This was about her, Monique Harper Staley, a woman who worked hard to get where she was in life and was working even harder to be a better person. Pastor Daniels made his choice and now she was making hers.

She called the family and told them about the celebration and how they were welcome to come be a part of it or not, it would happen either way. Some

Redemptive

questioned if it was appropriate to have her celebration on the same day of the pastor's funeral. The old Monique would have gone off at the implication, but the new Monique didn't care. For the first time in a very long time she was starting to feel the weight fall from her spirit and liked the freedom it was bringing. There was still a lot of work to do, but she really was trying to get to know the Lord on her own terms, not some box the religious folk were trying to put her in.

Each day leading up to the celebration, the media was playing up the life of Pastor Daniels. His wife and team obviously had gotten together and created a story that led to his suicide. It had nothing to do with the truth of what happened, and Monique knew it was to protect his legacy. She stopped watching the media hype not only for her sanity, but that part of her life was over and was choosing to put her energy into more positive things. The first thing on her list was to meet with Graham. After their divorce they'd remained friends as they continued to co-parent their children. Dr. Meyers advice on forgiveness made her realize there was some things she needed to get straight with him.

One night after work, she met Graham for a drink. She didn't explain over the phone to him why and he was always accommodating to anything she needed and agreed to meet. When they'd exchanged hellos, ordered their drinks and appetizers, Monique started the conversation.

"Graham, we went through a lot in our marriage and I blamed you for a lot of things, but what I didn't do was take the responsibility for my part in it."

"Where is this coming from, now after all these years?"

"I've gone through a lot over the last year and the incident in the woods caused me to remember something I blocked for years. I believe it has been the main reason for my behavior."

Graham sat with a puzzled look on his face but waited for her to continue.

"I was molested in my early teens by none other than Pastor Daniels."

"The man that just killed himself! Were you involved in what happened Moni?" asked Graham now with a look of concern.

"Yes, I mean no, not directly. I went to see him, but his wife blocked that. Apparently they'd been dealing with his nastiness for years and thought I was another one looking to extort money for my silence. Later that day, he came to the house asking for forgiveness."

Redemptive

"What? Where was Amar? How did he know where you lived?"

"Amar was there handling things. You know he's a big bully anyway. He was just waiting for something to pop off. You know we live in the internet age, where you can google anybody and anything. I'm sure that's what his assistant did."

The waiter came with the drinks and interrupted their conversation. They waited for him to leave before resuming. Monique looked around to see if anyone may be listening. She'd asked for a table in the back away from everybody, but the restaurant was starting to seat people where they were.

"I think he expected me to accept the forgiveness and go on with my life, so I told him I wasn't sure I could do that. He offered money, I refused. I think he felt backed into a corner. And guess what?"

"There's more?"

"He molested Cyrus too."

"Damn. That's messed up!

"For serious. I've been in counseling for months now trying to get my head together and I've learned a lot from the counselor, which is why I wanted to talk to you. I'm sorry for the way I was during the marriage.

The whole attitude of being in charge and getting you before you get me mindset. I now know it was me protecting myself from another man taking advantage of me."

"I didn't know, Moni and I'm sorry you went through that, but hey you survived it. Don't worry about us, we good and will always be. I'm glad you are getting the help you feel you need."

Graham reached for her hand, Monique put her hand in his and he gave it a squeeze. It was his way of assuring her he was in her corner and Monique felt the support he was giving her in his grip.

#####

Later when Monique arrived home Amar was sitting on the back patio drinking a beer with his feet up listening to music. Monique stood at the door before going out wondering what was on his mind. She was glad Amar came along in her life when he did. He was able to bring her what she needed in a relationship. Someone who supported her, and believed in her, and would take care of her. She was grateful for that. If she hadn't realized what that was before she did now……Blessed!

Chapter 26

The Celebration

The day of the celebration Monique could hardly contain herself. Life looked differently for her than it had in a long time. She'd had a good life, there was no question of that, but where she was now, couldn't compare. Something was happening to her and she couldn't explain it but was loving it. Best of all she knew it had nothing to do with Pastor Daniels.

She and Amar got up early in preparation for the day. Amar seasoned meats and veggies, while she made sure the house was in order. She then made different drinks, rinsed the dishes for the patio, checked the playlist, and made sure the outside icemaker was turned on.

Monique couldn't help but think about Shane and Tychia, whether they both would come or not. She so wanted them to be able to work things out, but that was between the two of them. If she hadn't learned anything else she was learning people have to take responsibility for their own actions. Her only job was to love and support them regardless which was more than enough.

After walking through the house one final time making sure everything was to her satisfaction, she went out to see if Amar needed any help. Monique checked the buffet table on the other side of where Amar was standing to make sure they were ready for the food once it came off the grill. Everything was in order and Monique when to change clothes. She decided to wear a soft yellow sundress to match her mood. Once she put it on and looked at the image in the mirror, Monique saw herself in a different light. "You've come a long way girl…..a mighty long way." Just as she slid her feet into her sandals, the doorbell rang.

When she answered the door, her grandma, aunts, and a couple of uncles were standing there. A few minutes later more family arrived, while others simply went straight to the back patio and made themselves at home. Family. You gotta love 'em. It wasn't long before everyone made their way outside except for Monique's grandma.

"Sit Moni, I want to talk to you for a minute."

Redemptive

"What is it grandma?" Monique asked as she sat.

"I guess you don't have to worry about Pastor Daniels now do you? He's standing before the Great Judge now. See sometimes you have to be still and let the Lord fight your battle."

Never wanting to disrespect her grandma, Monique struggled with how to answer her.

"Yes, grandma, but sometimes the devil will use you to try to escape what's coming to you."

"That's true too, but I believe the Lord prevailed in this one."

"Okay grandma. If that's what you believe."

"Keep living Moni, you'll see sometimes it's just best to leave things alone. I've been praying for his family. Them po people are having it hard right now, but God will comfort their heart."

Monique sat and listened to her grandma talk. She always thought her grandma was full of wisdom. This case was different and there was no need to argue about it, this was a day of celebration and she didn't need anything to change it.

"You look good grandma," Monique said while leaning over to kiss her on the cheek.

"Thanks baby. That yellow sholl look good on you. As a matter of fact, you glowin'. Whatcha been up to child?"

"Not much grandma, just trying to get my life together."

"That's all any of us can do is try, the rest is up to the good Lord."

"Hey, ya'll staying in the house all day? asked Aunt Sylvia as she entered the den where the two women sat.

"No, we just talking and catching up a bit. Who all out there?" Monique's grandma asked.

"Just about everybody," Aunt Sylvia answered.

"Good, said Monique, then it's a perfect time to give my speech! Come on let's go celebrate."

Monique helped her grandma up and the three women headed out back. Monique never liked being on the spot, but this new thing she was experiencing was giving her a boldness like she never had before. When they arrived outback, Aunt Sylvia was right, everybody was there including Shane and Tychia. Camille and the kids had arrived also. Monique made her rounds speaking to everybody, even Geneva.

Redemptive

When she finished she stood on her stepstool with a glass of wine in her hand.

"Can I have your attention please?" Amar turned the music off. Everyone immediately looked at Monique.

"Thank you all for coming here today. I don't want you to think this is a regular cookout where you just come and eat. Today I want to do something different. I want to talk about family and the importance of it. I know we cut up at times, sometimes we don't see eye to eye, but at the end of the day, we should still be there for one another.

I've had some changes in my life over the last several months starting with the accident on the walking trail. I don't think it was an accident now, I think it was to make me aware of life now and to embrace it, not what was." All Monique could see was about twenty sets of eyes looking at her confused. These people don't get it yet, she thought, but they will.

"Life is short and we can't keep wasting it on petty shi...stuff. I'm trying not to cuss....as much anyway. The family laughed at her self-correction.

Geneva, I want to start with you. I apologize for my anger toward you. Whether you get what I've been through is not important anymore, how I choose to deal with it is. We may not be best buds going forward, but I hold no ill will toward you.

Grandma, I love your wisdom and how you always tell me the truth, whether I want to hear it or not. You are the glue that holds our family together and you are loved and appreciated.

Aunt Sylvia, you are my best friend and confidant. My love for you is unending. Thank you for loving me for me.

Shane and Tychia. I'm glad to see you here, but I know you both have work to do if you want to save this marriage. But whether it works or not, find happiness in your life.

Cyrus, be free. Free from hiding in the shadows of your own life. Live it to the best of your ability and stop wondering what people are going to say. If you figure out what YOU want and chase it, you will be a much better person.

Amar, thank you for being my rock over these last several months. You told me at the beginning of this journey that you would support me and you have. I'm grateful to you. Love ya babe!

Secrets destroy families but the worst destruction is not allowing the person who is in pain or struggling to feel they don't have a safe place to fall. That's what family is for. If we say we love each other, then we should support one another. I love you all.......Now let's celebrate life!!!!

Redemptive

Amar was on cue with the music and each family member hugged Monique as they danced to the Cupid Shuffle.

The End

About the Author

Monica Hailey Sharpe is a woman of many interests. A native Charlottean, she is a wife, mother and grandmother. When Monica is not working in the business she co-owns with her husband Eddie, she likes to travel, shop, volunteer for missionary work, especially anything pertaining to the elderly and helping the homeless. Her heartbeat above all else is spending time with her four grandchildren.

Special Note

From Monica

Abuse in any form is never okay. My story although fictionalized in this book affected my life in so many ways.

For every person who is suffering in silence, you are not alone. Find the courage to talk to someone you can trust or seek counseling.

Please consider visiting my website for more information on how you can break the silence and connect with people who are willing to change the stigma that is attached to molestation, sexual abuse and assault.

www.monicahaileysharpe.com

Redemptive:

Freedom from the consequences of sin, evil and or suffering.

www.ingramcontent.com/pod-product-compliance
Lightning Source LLC
Chambersburg PA
CBHW051359290426
44108CB00015B/2085